KEY
PRAYERS

Volum

Daily Bible readings and prayer points
that will bless and increase your
individual and church
spiritual growth

Richard C Buxton

Unless otherwise indicated, biblical quotations are taken
from the New International Version © 1973, 1978, 1984
by the International Bible Society.

ISBN 978-0-9572515-0-2

Front cover design
DeLuxe Printers

Printed by
DeLuxe Printers
Acton Lane, London NW10 7NR, England
Tel: 020 8965 1771
Email: order@deluxeprinters.co.uk

Published by
R Buxton Publishing
Northfield Avenue, London W5 4UB, England
Tel: 020 8840 7508
Email: info@ecc.org.uk

DEDICATION

This book is dedicated to the army of inspiring men and women
who, down through the ages, have selflessly stood in the gap
between a sinful people and a holy and righteous God, and who
have passionately and persistently interceded for revival,
often at great cost, until it has come to pass;

to my wife, Rajinder, my soul mate and
faithful fellow minister in Christ;

and to all the prayer warriors, intercessors and members
of Ealing Christian Centre, drawn from the many nations
around the world, who together form our spiritual family in
Christ.

Revival Prayers - Volume 1

ACKNOWLEDGEMENTS

I am very grateful to Hakeem Kasumu, Jackie Raymond and Geraldine Blackwood for their unswerving support, help and expertise in the areas of printing and publishing; proofreading, copy editing and design; marketing and promotion (respectively), without whose time and enthusiastic encouragement, this book would never have been published.

REVIVAL PRAYERS - Volume 1

"This superb and powerful REVIVAL PRAYERS book is the result of consistency of faith and sound biblical foundations of Richard and Rajinder, the head ministers of Ealing Christian Centre in London. They were not only missionaries in Africa and Asia, but also founded the 24/7 Prayer Centre some ten years ago. I am so excited reading through the pages of this book and I intend to order copies for my church. Be prepared to join the PRAYER REVOLUTION sweeping across this nation."

Rev Major SAM LARBIE (Rtd)
Senior Minister, Elim Pentecostal Church, Camberwell, London

"The Lord has shown, through visions and prophecy, that the United Kingdom and indeed the world will witness a massive global revival. The volume you hold in your hands is an open door and portal connecting you with what God is doing on the Earth today. Get yourself, loved ones, church and community prepared! Prayer is the key weapon for victorious Christian living. I am confident that this book will charge your prayer batteries and give you a powerful spiritual LIFT!"

Rev Dr JONATHAN OLOYEDE
Team Leader, City Chapel and Convenor, GDOP (London)

Foreword

L ong before this book was ever written or conceived, had you had asked me to mention a significant church in Europe whose primary passion was prayer for revival, then my first thought would have centred upon Ealing Christian Centre (ECC).

From the first moment that Richard and Rajinder Buxton came to London in 1997, this was to become a foundational principle of a vision that was to propel ECC to become one of the largest and most significant churches in the capital.

There is an aspiration in many Christians to discover 'the next new thing' that God wants them to experience. However, while spiritual ambition is to be commended, the energy expended in such an endeavour should not be at the expense of overlooking what God has already asked us to accomplish.

> ... the energy expended ... should not be at the expense of overlooking what God has already asked us to accomplish

If a person goes to their doctor complaining of chest pains, he or she may well advise them to watch their weight, eat more healthily and exercise more. If they visit their GP subsequently - with the same condition - and ask for fresh advice, their physician is likely to say, "I have nothing new to say to you until you have complied with what I have already instructed."

A desire for revival is similar. God will not offer palatable shortcuts or remedies for a broken world, until we have first undertaken the hard work of tenacious intercession. Our Western Christian worldview too easily sees God as a 'Cosmic Aspirin', a vehicle whose purpose - it appears - is to remove all aspects of struggle and pain. It perceives humankind as the centre of the universe, and something upon which Heaven should meticulously dance attendance. It all too often embraces the theology of the spoilt child that must have its needs met – and met instantly.

Yet we all know that it is the purposes of God that are the axis around which everything is to move. Our role as the Church is to align ourselves with the gravitational pull of Almightiness – to stay within the orbit of His objectives, and move within the trajectory of His divine decrees. The only way that the world can harmoniously work is when it revolves around the Son. Prayer and intercession adjust our flight path to the will of God and, in doing so, our navigational GPS becomes the mind and influence of the Holy Spirit, rather than the will and inclinations of our human hearts.

The first focus of revival is the Church and not the world. You can only revive that which once was full of life. Plans, programmes, reconstituted church and good intention are totally devoid of the necessary energy. Revival emanates only through a spiritual dynamic, and that dynamic is only released through intercessory prayer. My problem is not in learning that I need to pray more - I already know that. My problem is that I need to pray *better*. The disciples understood that too, and that is why they asked the Lord in Luke 11:1 that He might "teach them to pray".

What you are about to encounter in the pages that follow is a way to pray better, dig deeper

God will not offer palatable shortcuts or remedies for a broken world, until we have first undertaken the hard work of tenacious intercession

and climb higher. It is a tool that I will want to use, and I encourage you to join me in the journey. It is an adventure, but not one that is without its challenges. Mountain top views are not usually embraced without a need to climb. Victory is only experienced through the process of battle.

We are indebted to Richard Buxton for facilitating this, and for helping us to be far better equipped so that, when it comes to interceding for a revival, we become a Church that is fully 'fit for purpose'.

Rev John Glass
General Superintendent
Elim Pentecostal Churches

EALING CHRISTIAN CENTRE supports a number of missionaries and overseas missions in different countries around the globe. Profits from the sale of this book will go towards the support of such missions.

Illustration by artist Mark Dishley
© Mark Dishley 2012
Email: markdishley@yahoo.co.uk

Contents

INTRODUCTION

This is a book for those who have a passion to see revival in our nation. It is for those who are prepared to set aside time daily to humble themselves and pray, and seek the face of God in repentance, turning from all ungodly ways, and interceding to the "Judge of all the Earth" to forgive the sins of our nation and to send revival.

By revival, I mean in its simplest sense of 'to come alive again', that is 'to revivify'. It is possible for a person to be in a coma; they are alive and breathing, but make no contribution and have no positive influence on those around them. The Church can be like that, alive – just – but having no positive impact on the society in which it exists, with the result that the society descends into an increasingly downward spiral. This has been the story of our society over the past decades. The Church can exist, but without living in the abundance of life and the fullness of the power of the Holy Spirit that Jesus came to bring to us.

The Church can exist, but without living in the abundance of life and the fullness of the power of the Holy Spirit ...

Jesus, the Son of God, left Heaven's glory and, at the incarnation, took on humanity, leaving aside his divine powers for the season he was on earth. Instead, he relied solely on the Holy Spirit working in and through him.

"Your attitude should be the same as that of Christ Jesus: Who, being in very nature God, did not consider equality with God something to be grasped, but made himself nothing, taking the very nature of a servant, being made in human likeness. And being found in appearance as a man, he humbled himself

It is possible to be spiritually alive ... but having no impact on anyone or anything around us

and became obedient to death – even death on a cross!" (Philippians 2:5-8).

The reality is that when we look at Jesus of Nazareth living a sinless life; living in conformity to the ways of a righteous God, and moving in all the miraculous gifts of the Holy Spirit, we see what, in God's purpose, a normal human being should be like. The fact that we may see ourselves as so different merely demonstrates how far short of the glory of God human beings have fallen.

But we are justified through our faith in the finished work of Christ through the cross and resurrection; we receive the Holy Spirit into our lives the moment we are born again, enabling us to develop the fruit of the Spirit (Galatians 5:22-23), and we can be baptised in the Holy Spirit in order to move in the nine supernatural gifts of the Spirit (Acts 8:14-17, 1 Corinthians 12:7-11).

It is possible to be spiritually alive – just – but having no impact on anyone or anything around us; not seeking or using what God has made available to us – the power of a godly life and his Holy Spirit. "But you will receive power when the Holy Spirit comes on you; and you will be my witnesses..." (Acts 1:8). Revival starts in the heart and life of the believer. First must come that desire for personal revival; a desire to walk in the pathways of righteousness, to "...continue to work out your salvation with fear and trembling, for it is God who works in you to will and to act according to his good purpose" (Philippians 2:12-13).

When we truly understand what we have been saved from; what it cost our God to save us, and what we have been saved to, it will surely evoke the same response as Isaiah who, when he fully grasped these truths through the vision he saw, dedicated the rest of his life thereafter to obeying the Word of the Lord and seeking to bring change to his society (Isaiah 6:1-13).

When the Church experiences revival, it will be on fire to take out the Gospel in evangelistic power in all its Holy Spirit fullness, asking people the question: "Will you receive Christ as your Saviour and Lord?" When God himself moves in revival, the power of his awesome holy presence reverses the situation, so that people are convicted to come and ask: "What must I do to be saved?"

Firstly, this book is for those who are seeking to grow closer to God in character, in holiness and in Christlikeness. This is always the first priority, to "...seek first his Kingdom and his righteousness..." (Matthew 6:33).

Secondly, it is for those who long to see a visitation of God once more in our nation. Revival starts in the life of the believer, that is, it starts in the Church. When individual believers come alive again with the fullness of the abundance of the life that comes from Christ and the Holy Spirit, and the Church starts to live that life and take it outside the confines of the church building into every area of society, where those individual believers live and work, they can then begin to bring change to each level of society they spend their time in.

We are exhorted to "...fan into flame the gift of God which is in you..."(2 Timothy 1:6), the gifts that are given for the purpose of service, primarily in the workplace and marketplace, the home and the neighbourhoods. We are called upon to pray; we are also called upon to act. The two must go hand in hand.

This book is a book of daily prayers. All the prayers are based on Scripture – the principle being: if we are praying according to the Word of God, we are unlikely to be praying amiss, which James tells us is possible. "When you ask, you do not receive, because you ask with the wrong motives..." (James 4:3).

At Ealing Christian Centre, we prioritise prayer. We also emphasise that every believer is a minister (ie. servant) for Christ; called upon to be his ambassador in every stratum of society where we each find ourselves on a daily basis. We are to live out what we believe, and allow the life of Christ within us to overflow to influence those around us as the salt and light Jesus has called us to be - witnesses for Jesus in word and in deed. My vision is to see revival in the Church that will then overflow into the communities around us.

If we are praying according to the Word of God, we are unlikely to be praying amiss

For this purpose, for a number of years I have written such daily prayer points, which are distributed to the whole church. For those who gather for our two daily prayer meetings – morning and evening – in the church, these intercessors use them to pray. For those who cannot, they can be used at home. In

We must be actively seeking to create the environment for revival to happen

this way, each one can be praying and interceding together daily with one accord, even if we are not all physically present in one group.

In June 2002, we set up a 24-hour Prayer Centre and, for 24 hours a day, 365 days a year ever since, it has been manned by intercessors. There is a continual uprising of prayer that goes from the church. They pray for revival and for the many prayer requests that are sent in. The Prayer Centre has telephone lines, and people (locally, from around the country and from overseas) phone in their prayer requests which are prayed for by the intercessors. Many amazing answers to prayer are fed back to us each week.

If we are praying for revival, we must be actively seeking to create the environment for it to happen. Prayer and evangelism go together, and we have experienced a significant increase in effectiveness in our regular church evangelism since the church began 24/7 prayer. Whereas previously, people would not stop to listen, now we find them open – to the point that salvations and healings take place on our streets on a regular basis.

In this book, there are five prayer points for each day. Mostly they are in the first person plural ('we' and 'us') in line with how Jesus taught us to pray in the 'Lord's Prayer'. Each month, the prayers are based on a different passage of Scripture. As we pray through the prayer points, we are asking God to change us in line with his Word, and also we are interceding for our society. As we understand more fully who we are in Christ; how we are to live our lives, and what we are to do to influence others around us, we are seeking to live out what we are praying for – revival; revival in us and revival in our nation.

My prayer is that this will lead us closer to God in experience, in character and in power – in short, to enable us to be more like Jesus, and to experience the abundance of the new life he has given us, which enables us to make a positive and lasting impact on all those we meet with daily.

Richard C Buxton

January

Living as Children of God
Matthew Chapters 5 to 7

As we begin the year, we start this month by praying through what is popularly known as "The Sermon on the Mount", which comprises three chapters where Jesus expounds the principles for the Kingdom of God, or the Kingdom of Heaven. He starts by giving a detailed description of what a citizen of the Kingdom of God is like. Rather than describing different sets of people, the nine descriptions starting with the word "blessed" (or "The Beatitudes", as they are called) are different aspects of the same person, namely the character of one who is truly a citizen of God's Kingdom, that is, the true follower of Christ.

So, blessed are the persons who, recognising their own personal spiritual poverty, mourn for their sin, that is, they repent and are comforted by finding salvation in Christ. With the help of the Holy Spirit now within them, they can start to exhibit the characteristics of Christ, namely meekness; a hungering and thirsting after righteousness; a new character which practises mercy, and which is pure in heart, seeking to be a peacemaker in a troubled world.

> **With the help of the Holy Spirit ... they can start to exhibit the characteristics of Christ**

The citizens of the Kingdom of God can be noted by their different character, attitude and values

With a character now so unlike what the world is used to, such a person will be persecuted, insulted and slandered. But, knowing they have received the full quality of eternal life that starts now and continues, beyond death, in the presence of God, such citizens of God's Kingdom can remain joyful, understanding that the trials of this present world are not worthy to be compared with the glory that is to come.

Instead, the citizens of the Kingdom of God now belong to two kingdoms: they live as subjects to the higher divine laws of God, but physically they currently are in a fallen world, where they are called upon to exhibit the righteousness of God's Kingdom; to be salt in a rotting society, and light to those in spiritual darkness.

The citizens of the Kingdom of God can be noted by their different character, attitude and values. So they will not let their anger remain unbridled, but instead will seek to right wrongs and bring about reconciliation in relationships. They will not follow the world in engaging in fornication or adultery, either in deed or in thought. They remain committed for life to their wives or husbands; can be trusted to keep their word, and can demonstrate the *agapé* love of God which forgives even enemies. They love to give generously, knowing their true treasures are in Heaven; seek God in prayer and fasting; trust God with their earthly concerns; do not act like hypocrites, but are transparent and honest, with the wisdom to build their lives on the foundations of Christ's teachings.

This month, we are praying to be able to grow to become more like such a character which, in reality, is the character of Christ.

· · · · · · · · · · · · · · · · · ·

1st Matthew 5:1-4
Becoming Christlike (1)

1. Lord, help us to always remember that all that we are - and all that we have - comes from you, and that without you we are nothing, so that pride has no place in our lives.
2. Lord, cause us to realise that in you we have everything that belongs to our God, since we are heirs of God and joint heirs with Christ.
3. Cause us, Lord, to live at all times in a way that befits the citizens of the Kingdom of Heaven.
4. May we experience the blessedness that comes from mourning for our sinful nature, knowing that, in Christ, we find the comfort of the forgiveness of sins.
5. Thank you, Lord Jesus, for the eternal blessedness that we experience when we mourn for our sins, repent and find salvation through your finished work on the cross.

2nd Matthew 5:5-8
Becoming Christlike (2)

1. Teach us, O Lord, the difference between meekness and weakness, so that we learn how to exhibit meekness from a position of strength.
2. Cause us to hunger and thirst after righteousness, and may we continually be filled to overflowing with the Holy Spirit.
3. Give us hearts of compassion in all our dealings with people, so that we exhibit to others the same measure of mercy that you show us, O God.
4. Give us clean hands and a pure heart, O Lord, so that we always feel comfortable coming into your presence.
5. Reveal to us more of yourself this day, Lord, we ask.

3rd   Matthew 5:9-10
Becoming Christlike (3)

1. Teach us the difference between peace*keeping* and peace*making*, O Lord, and may we be people who actively seek to bring reconciliation at all times.
2. For any amongst us who currently have problems with a personal relationship, help them to actively seek to restore and mend what has been broken.
3. Help us to be people who actively seek to help non-believers to make their peace with God, through repentance and faith in Christ.
4. Cause us to remember, Lord Jesus, that you are the Prince of Peace, and as we seek to be peacemakers, we are becoming more like the Son of God.
5. Now that we have Christ within our lives, make us noticeably different as we seek to avoid being divisive, but rather to live peaceably with all people.

4th   Matthew 5:11-12
Rejoicing amidst adversity

1. Help us realise, Lord, that following you in this fallen world is bound to bring us into conflict with those who reject you; may we not be discouraged when that happens.
2. Keep our eyes fixed upon our final destiny, which is eternity in your presence, O Lord, so that our hearts may constantly rejoice.
3. We pray for all amongst us who are experiencing times of difficulty because of those who dislike the fact they are Christians; strengthen them, O Lord, and let them experience your joy.
4. We pray for all those amongst us who are under pressure in places of work because it is hostile to practising Christians; show them your divine favour, O God.

5. We pray for all those who are actively hostile to those in the church simply because they are following Christ; open their eyes and save them, O Lord.

5th Matthew 5:13-15
Being salt and light

1. Help us keep our cutting edge as followers of Christ, so that we remain influencers of others and not the other way round.
2. Lead us to someone today who we can influence for Christ, we pray.
3. May our characters be such that even without words we can influence someone for Christ today.
4. Cause our thoughts to remain focused on that which is good and positive, so that anything which comes from 'darkness' can never bring us down.
5. Place your people in every position of influence throughout our land, O Lord, from the highest to the humblest positions.

6th Matthew 5:16-20
Living out the Gospel

1. Let our light so shine before men, O Lord, that they may see our godly acts and praise our Father in Heaven.
2. Help us to walk closely to you, O God, so that we do not consciously or carelessly sin.
3. May your Word be hidden in our hearts, O Lord, so that we always know the right choices to make.
4. Teach us, we pray, to reverence your ways, so that we never become complacent, but daily live in the righteous fear of the Lord.
5. May we never be tempted to trust in our own righteousness, but only to trust wholly in you, Lord Jesus.

 Matthew 5:21-22
Overcoming anger

1. Teach us the difference between righteous anger and selfish anger, recognising that when we get angry it is more likely to spring from selfishness; help us to change.
2. If we are harbouring unforgiveness towards anyone, help us, Holy Spirit, to extend the forgiveness that comes from the *agapé* love of God within us.
3. Stir within us the righteous anger that hates sin, injustice and unrighteousness, so that we may be motivated to intercessory prayer and godly action.
4. Help us to put a guard on our lips, O Lord, so that we always think before we speak words we may later regret.
5. Help us to always speak words that build others up, and not cut them down.

 Matthew 5:23-26
Living in harmony

1. Cause us to remember, O Lord, that we cannot truly worship you if we are carrying grudges against others; enable us to put things right, we pray.
2. Teach us how to ignore offences to us that only hurt our pride but have no further consequence, so that we are not eaten up with inner anger.
3. We pray for all husbands and wives in the church, O Lord; may they learn how to deal quickly with offences and so resolve them at an early stage.
4. We pray for all parents and their children in the church, O Lord; may they learn to quickly resolve differences, so that family unity may be maintained.
5. Cause each of us within the church to quickly resolve any differences that may arise between us, so that the unity of the Spirit is maintained, we pray.

9th Matthew 5:27-30
Purity

1. Give us the wisdom, desire and strength not to commit fornication, we pray.
2. Keep us from the folly of adultery, O Lord, which helps no-one but harms man, woman and family.
3. For those struggling with unwanted homosexual desires, strengthen them with your peace and love, O Lord, that will help them not to cross your boundaries.
4. For any struggling with the bondage of pornography, help them to seek help and counsel to break free from its ruinous effects, we pray.
5. Help us at all times to bring all our thoughts into captivity to Christ, we pray.

10th Matthew 5:31-32
Praying for marriages

1. Help each Christian husband in the church to remain obedient to you, O Lord, so that he always loves his wife as Christ loves the Church.
2. Help each Christian wife in the church to remain obedient to you, O Lord, and give her husband the respect you require.
3. For any marriages in the church that are under strain and are heading towards divorce, bring the husband and wife to the place of repentance and mutual forgiveness, we pray.
4. We pray for all the marriages of those we know who are not Christians; strengthen them in their relationships, and help them to remain committed to each other throughout their lives.
5. We pray that in our nation, all people would come to realise the folly of marginalising marriage, but recognise the wisdom of God in living within a covenant of marriage.

 Matthew 5:33-37
Keeping our word

1. May we be people who are always trustworthy in all that we say and do, O Lord.
2. May we be people who are faithful in our places of work, arriving on time, not leaving early, and fulfilling our responsibilities as unto the Lord.
3. When we commit ourselves with a promise to do something, may we realise that we are accountable to you, O God, to fulfil our word.
4. In the work we commit ourselves to do in your church, O Lord, help us to see it as a first priority to be fulfilled, and not as a secondary after-thought.
5. Help us to daily fulfil the promise we made when we asked Christ to be our Lord as well as our Saviour; indeed, be the Lord of every part of our lives, Lord Jesus.

 Matthew 5: 38-42
Going the extra mile

1. Always cause us to remember your words, O God, that it is yours to avenge, not ours; give us the grace not to retaliate to provocation.
2. Give us generous hearts just like yours, Lord Jesus.
3. May our first inclination be to say "Yes" rather than "No" to those who seek our help.
4. Help us to be generous with our time, O Lord, giving of our time to you and to others.
5. May we be generous with our finances, O Lord, giving selflessly where and when we are able to.

Matthew 5:43-45
Loving the unlovely

1. May we be a people who experience hate only for the sin, but never for the sinner.
2. Help us to realise that, since we have the Holy Spirit within us, we are quite capable of loving the unlovely, including those who regard us as enemies.
3. Help us to develop the *agapé* love of God within us, which enables us to love people despite of who they are.
4. Lord, help us to be fair and even-handed to all people at all times, not favouring one above the other just because we like them more.
5. Lord, we pray right now for everyone who treats us badly; bless them, and cause them to experience your grace and forgiveness.

Matthew 5:46-48
Be like God

1. Lord, help us to be different from those who do not know you, because we bear the characteristics of our Heavenly Father.
2. Help us to understand the depravity of sin, just like you do, O God, and so hate to be tainted by it.
3. Help us to love just like you do, O Lord.
4. Help us to seek the good in others, just like you do, O Lord, seeking to help them fulfil their best.
5. Help us to be willing to lay down our lives in every situation, just like Jesus, we pray.

15th Matthew 6:1-4
Giving

1. Cause us to give simply because we want others to be blessed, O Lord.
2. Give us hearts that willingly are able to let go of money selflessly, we pray.
3. May we never neglect to give our tithes to you, O Lord, so that it can be used to further the ministries that cause people to be saved, discipled and grow in Christ.
4. When you bless us financially above what we need, give us the generosity to give to you offerings, over and above our tithes, we pray.
5. Teach us to understand and operate our finances according to your principles of sowing and reaping, O Lord, realising that we reap according to how we sow.

16th Matthew 6:5-6
Prayerful lives

1. Lord, teach us to pray.
2. Train us in the ability to live a lifestyle of prayer, knowing how to call on you at any time of the day or night, and in any circumstance.
3. Teach us how to live constantly conscious of your presence within and around us, O Lord.
4. May our first thought in the morning and our last thought at night be of you, O God.
5. Teach us how to pray selflessly, O Lord.

17th Matthew 6:7-8
Praying with faith

1. Teach us to pray always according to your will, O God, and not according to our will alone.

2. When we pray, give us the faith to believe that we will receive.
3. Show us when we need to keep persevering in prayer, and when we can leave it at your throne, knowing the work of prayer is accomplished for that situation.
4. Holy Spirit, guide us in how we should pray and what for, so that we may work in partnership with you in prayer.
5. Help us to learn how to pray with a faith that can move mountains, O Lord.

18th Matthew 6:9-13
The Lord's Prayer (1)

1. Our Father in Heaven, may our lips always demonstrate our reverence for your holy Name.
2. May the actions that we carry out always be in keeping with a reverence for the holy God whom we serve.
3. Let your Kingdom come amongst us even now, Lord Jesus, by your people living their lives like Christ, and exercising all the gifts of the Holy Spirit.
4. Let your Kingdom come on earth, Lord Jesus, by enabling us to lead many people to salvation, having the Kingdom reign of Christ in their hearts.
5. Lord Jesus, we look forward to and pray for your physical return to this earth to set up your Kingdom to rule over all the world.

19th Matthew 6:9-13
The Lord's Prayer (2)

1. For all the necessities we need today, O Lord, please provide for us.
2. For all those we know who are in need, help them also today and, if necessary, help them through us.
3. We forgive right now all who have hurt us, to the same extent that you have forgiven us, O Lord.

4. Guard our hearts and our minds, Heavenly Father, so that the devil may not have any foothold in our lives.
5. Cause us to shake off, right now, any foothold or fingerhold we have allowed the devil to have in our lives or in our minds, we pray.

20th Matthew 6:14-15
Forgiving

1. Heavenly Father, help us not to bring ourselves into self-condemnation by holding on to unforgiveness.
2. Help us to understand that forgiveness is a decision of the mind and will, not merely an emotion of the heart, so that holding unforgiveness therefore becomes disobedience to you, O Lord.
3. For those who have hurt us so badly that it is humanly difficult to forgive, what we cannot do by our human nature cause us to do through our new spiritual nature.
4. Help us to note the seriousness of your words, Lord Jesus, that if we do not forgive, we are not forgiven; cause us to act.
5. Help us, Holy Spirit, at all times to remain in an attitude of forgiveness to all people.

21st Matthew 6:16-18
Fasting

1. Teach us, Holy Spirit, to learn the value of fasting with prayer.
2. Give us the desire to fast and the wisdom to carry it out, O Lord.
3. Show us when you want us to fast, and the specific, strategic, spiritual purposes for fasting at that time, we pray.
4. Help us to overcome great spiritual opposition through fasting and prayer, we pray.
5. Make us a people who are spiritually strong, because we understand and use the spiritual weapons of prayer, fasting and God's Word to overcome the powers of darkness.

 Matthew 6:19-23
True riches

1. Keep our priorities in true perspective, O Lord, recognising that we are on this earth for only a brief period of time.
2. Show us how to store up treasures in Heaven, O God, so that we are always spiritually rich.
3. Help us to use our worldly riches in ways that produce spiritual riches also.
4. Whilst thanking you, O Lord, for all we own, help us to have a light hold on them, remembering that the things of this world have only fleeting value.
5. May our eyes always be beholding that which is good and pure, so that our bodies do not become tainted with darkness.

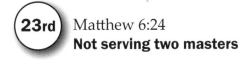 Matthew 6:24
Not serving two masters

1. Keep us from compromising with the ways of the world, O Lord, so that we do not end up trying to serve two masters.
2. Keep our love for you, O Lord, pure and unadulterated.
3. May our passion for you only ever grow, O God, as we continually seek to stir up the spiritual flames already within us.
4. Help us to continually keep our old nature crucified, so that our new spiritual nature may flourish.
5. If we are serving you with less than the zeal you deserve, O Lord, bring us to our knees in repentance and change our attitudes, we pray.

24th Matthew 6:25-32
Don't worry

1. Teach us a trust in you, O Lord, that helps us to learn how not to worry.
2. Holy Spirit, may we allow you to develop within us more of the fruit of the Spirit, including peace.
3. Help us to remember every testimony from our past, when we have seen you provide for us; as we do so, may we realise that you can do it again and again.
4. Teach us, O God, that our faith is only developed and built up in those times when we need to trust you for things we are lacking; help us to grow spiritually at such times.
5. Help us to remember your Word, O Lord, which says, "If God be for us then who can be against us?" Why then should we worry?

25th Matthew 6:33-34
Seeking his Kingdom first

1. Lord, move our hearts to continually seek first your Kingdom and your righteousness.
2. Let not our hearts grow cold, O Lord, and if they already are, then help us to see the seriousness of our spiritual condition, bringing us to our knees to seek you.
3. Teach us, Holy Spirit, that being like Jesus is the first priority you have for each of our lives, and you desire our co-operation in that changing process.
4. Cause us, Holy Spirit, to desire the best spiritual gifts, so that we can fulfil Christ's commission to us to preach the Gospel; heal the sick; drive out demons, and speak in new tongues.
5. May your Kingdom come and your will be done, in every part of our individual lives, O God.

 Matthew 7:1-6
Removing hypocrisy

1. Help us not to be hypocrites, O Lord.

2. Convict us, Holy Spirit, so that we are the first to be conscious of the fact that we have failings in our lives and characters, and help us put things right.
3. Keep us from having a critical spirit towards others, O Lord, especially since that often goes hand in hand with an inability to see our own shortcomings.
4. Help us to understand the seriousness of your words, O Lord, that "in the same way you judge others, you will be judged", so that we may treat others with mercy.
5. Help us to treasure all that is sacred, O God, never treating lightly that which you desire us to value highly.

 Matthew 7:7-9
Ask, seek, knock

1. Teach us, Holy Spirit, what to ask for and how to ask for it, as we come to our God in prayer.
2. Give us the desire to seek out from you, O God, everything that you want to give us, but for which you first want to see our earnest and genuine desire to receive.
3. May we be a people who understand that there are times when we need to keep knocking in prayer until we see the breakthrough and the door opened.
4. May we not be deterred from asking from you the best you have to give us, O Lord, since you have told us that you desire to give good gifts to those who ask you.
5. Lord, we pray for an open door of revival; start in our individual lives, and spread through your Church to our city and nation, we pray.

 Matthew 7:10-12
The Golden Rule

1. Teach us to be selfless, O God.
2. Teach us to love others as we would have them love us, we pray.
3. Teach us to speak the words of encouragement and blessing to others that we are grateful to receive for ourselves.
4. Teach us to be generous in our acts of kindness to others, O Lord.
5. As we sow the love of God all around us, may we reap the harvest of God's love in every part of our lives, we pray.

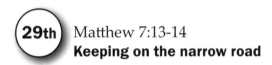 Matthew 7:13-14
Keeping on the narrow road

1. Lord, keep our feet from wandering off the pathway of righteousness and holiness, as we hear your voice in our minds saying, "This is the way, walk in it."
2. If we are carrying too much baggage of the world to be able to fit through the narrow gate, help us to shed everything that hinders our passing into the fullness of the presence of God.
3. Help us to guide people from the wide road that leads to destruction onto the narrow road that leads to eternal life, we pray.
4. We pray for all those who are close to us, who we know are still on the wide road to destruction; save them, we pray.
5. We pray for any in the church who are in danger of leaving the narrow road for reasons of discouragement, backsliding, or being attracted by the world; guard them from falling, we pray.

30th Matthew 7:15-23
True relationship with God

1. Give us the wisdom and discernment not to be led astray by false teaching, whether in church, through individuals, or through the media.
2. God forbid that we should be found to be false teachers of the Word of God; rather, cause us to work out our salvation with fear and trembling, we pray.
3. Cause us to remember that the fruit of the Spirit is the true test of Christlikeness and not our gifts, talents or demonstrations of power.
4. When we call you "Lord", may that not be a glib statement, but a true reflection of our yieldedness to you and to your will, in every area of our lives, O God.
5. Keep us close to your presence, O Lord, and may we remain near to your very heartbeat, we pray.

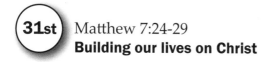

31st Matthew 7:24-29
Building our lives on Christ

1. Give us the wisdom, O God, to build every part of our lives on the solid Rock of Christ.
2. May we obediently bring every aspect of our personal lives under the authority of your words, Lord Jesus.
3. May every part of our lives - at school, college, the office, the factory, or any other workplace - be placed squarely on the foundation of the words of Christ.
4. May our homes be places where every aspect of our domestic lives are firmly set on the foundation of the words of Christ.
5. Cause our church, in every area of its life, work, ministry and vision, to be solidly based, rooted and set on nothing other than the very words of Christ, its Rock.

" Lord, as the calm, blue skies
are above every storm,
help us to look up beyond
any momentary trouble
to the One who is
calmly watching from above. **"**

(February 7)

February

The Pathway to Victory
Joshua Chapters 1 to 8

It seemed like a daunting task that lay ahead for Joshua. With Moses now dead, he had been entrusted with the responsibility to lead the two million or so Israelites into the final phase of their journey. He had been entrusted to lead them into victory.

He had some good qualifications for being a spiritual leader; he had been a faithful servant for forty years, attending to the needs of Moses. Many of the great men of God in the Bible learned the development of character from servanthood that enabled them to become men who could be used by God. They had no inflated sense of their own importance, and had learned to trust not in their own ability, but in the God who could do all things. Men like Joseph, David, Elisha and supremely the Son

Many of the great men of God in the Bible learned the development of character from servanthood

Joshua's success would come from being familiar with the Word of God

of God himself, who showed us that servant leadership is God's most powerful instrument to accomplish his plans on earth.

Joshua knew how to wait patiently on the Lord and for the Lord. Twice he had had to wait for forty days part-way up Mount Sinai, while Moses went to the top and stayed in the presence of God. While the people below got bored and backslid, saying that Moses had disappeared, Joshua just waited as he had been told. While Aaron was succumbing to the pressure from the people to compromise, Joshua was quiet before the Lord, waiting on him.

The first chapter clearly shows us that Joshua was anxious about the responsibility of his God-given role, as God keeps telling him to be strong and courageous. His success would come from being familiar with the Word of God, upon which he was to meditate continually, so that he could put its principles into practice in daily life. He learned how to see miracles happen, but not until the step of faith had been taken; the flooded Jordan River would dry up, in order for them to cross, only when the priests' feet actually stepped into its flowing waters. The walls of Jericho would fall, but only as Joshua faithfully carried out God's unusual instructions, which defied any known battle plan.

Joshua would learn how sin in the camp can bring the move of God to an abrupt halt until it was confronted, rooted out and holiness restored. His faith would rise to the level where he could confidently and publicly call on God to cause the sun to stop in the sky, so that he could complete the victory God had handed to him.

As we pray through the Book of Joshua this month, we are praying that God would help instil in us all those qualities that will enable us to be instruments through which the Lord can work, to see us, the Church, move into a place of spiritual and practical victory.

• • • • • • • • • • • • • • • • •

1st Joshua 1:1-2
Moses is dead - Taking personal responsibility

1) Lord, thank you for the generation before us and all we learned from them; give each of us the maturity to take up their mantle of responsibility for ourselves.
2) Reveal to me the personal responsibilities you have called me to fulfil in your Church and for your Kingdom.
3) Give me a totally willing heart to accept and act upon what you have called me to do.
4) Thank you that we are all called to be ministers for Christ; help us to understand the high calling of living for Jesus.
5) Arouse your Church to rise to the challenge of living for Jesus in this, our own present generation.

2nd Joshua 1:3-4
Enlarging the territory

1) Lord, you have said you will build your Church; may we be willing helpers.
2) Give your Church in this nation and worldwide, a vision and strategy for growth, and not for just defending the status quo.
3) Raise up your people to all manner of positions of influence in our society.
4) Raise up your people to positions in every level of government.
5) Help your Church to reach out, in all manner of ways, to all who are lost, and bring them into your Kingdom.

3rd Joshua 1:5
Remembering who is with us constantly

1) Thank you, Lord, for your promise that you will never leave nor forsake us.

2) When you allow us to go through times of trial, help us to remember that you will never leave nor forsake us.
3) In our weakness you are our strength; strengthen us for the tasks of today, O Lord.
4) Cause us to remember that we can do all things through Christ who strengthens us.
5) Even though I walk through the valley of death, I will fear no evil, for you are with me.

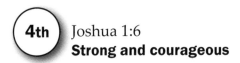

4th — Joshua 1:6
Strong and courageous

1) Help us always to let the light of our Christian witness burn brightly.
2) May we not be intimidated by those who oppose Christ and the ways of God, and give us strength when we are in such circumstances.
3) As we daily seek to grow closer to you, strengthen our spiritual life that will cause us to become bold and strong.
4) Lord, reveal to each of us our weak points, and give us grace to grow in strength instead.
5) Teach us to fear God, but not to fear man.

5th — Joshua 1:7
Careful to obey

1) Lord, since you have said "Obedience is better than sacrifice", strengthen the desire within us to obey you at all times.
2) Forgive us for any and every act of disobedience, and give us the determination to always walk in obedience.
3) Lord, may we be careful to obey all your Word, and not just the parts we choose.
4) Teach us to appreciate that obedience brings the full blessing of God in our lives.

5) Strengthen our desire to know your Word fully, that we may be able to obey all your ways.

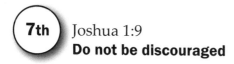

6th Joshua 1:8
Prosperity through obedience

1) Lord, cause us to remember that we are to be ambassadors for Jesus at all times, and may we daily affect all those, with whom we come into contact, with the power of the Gospel.
2) May we be people of the Word; ones who read, meditate and act in obedience to your Word at all times.
3) As we walk in obedience, prosper your people, O Lord, that out of our prosperity we can be a blessing to you and to many others.
4) As your people walk in obedience to you, prosper their lives, their homes, their jobs, their businesses and, above all, their ministries – that you may be glorified.
5) Forgive all our acts of disobedience and, as we walk according to your ways, bring a success that will, in turn, bring influence for good and for God in our society.

7th Joshua 1:9
Do not be discouraged

1) When the wind and the storm seem strong around us, help us to keep our eyes fixed on you, Lord Jesus.
2) Why are you downcast, O my soul? Why so disturbed within me? Put your hope in God.
3) Lord, as the calm, blue skies are above every storm, help us to look up beyond any momentary trouble to the One who is calmly watching from above.
4) Give each of us the ministry of encouragement, and lead us today to someone who will be strengthened by our words of encouragement.

5) Lord, you are the Creator and Sustainer of this immeasurably vast universe; help us to keep our comparatively little problems in proportion, and to trust in your strength.

8th — Joshua 1:10-15
Help your brothers

1) Cause us, O Lord, to remember that your Church is a body that is dependent upon each part working for the good of the whole.
2) Help me to make a difference and create a lasting impact on someone else today.
3) Help us to experience the truth that it is more blessed to give than to receive; may we be givers in every way to God and to others.
4) Take away any feeling of jealousy or insecurity at the abilities of others, that we may help one another in God's Kingdom to the best of our ability.
5) Whatever we do, teach us to realise that we do it for you, and let everything be done as a sacrifice for you.

9th — Joshua 1:16-18
Obedience to God's appointed leaders

1) Lord, you appoint your leaders; we pray that you would give them all the strength, courage, wisdom and boldness they need to fulfil their God-given tasks.
2) In accordance with your will, may we make their task easier by giving them our full support.
3) Give us an open and humble heart to receive correction if and whenever that is necessary, that we may grow in all your ways.
4) We pray for all those in positions of leadership in the church – pastors, elders, teachers, Discipleship Cell leaders and others. Bless them, and may we be a blessing to them.
5) Expose and reveal any acts of rebellion within us, that we may repent and not be a hindrance to your work.

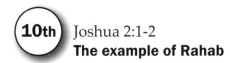

10th Joshua 2:1-2
The example of Rahab

1) Lord, we pray for any in the church who are in sexual sin; open their eyes to the harm they are doing to themselves, to the other person, and to their relationship with you.
2) We pray for all the young people in the church; guard them from the harmful teachings, pressures and ways of the world.
3) We pray for our society that has made an idol out of sex, with disastrous social consequences; open their eyes to the folly of such ways.
4) As Rahab turned to the Lord when she met some of God's people, may we be instrumental in bringing many to Christ who are currently far from him.
5) Thank you, Lord, that for all who turn wholeheartedly to you, they can become a brand new person - the old has gone and the new has come.

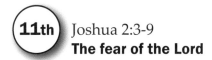

11th Joshua 2:3-9
The fear of the Lord

1) May we constantly remember, as Rahab learned, that the fear of the Lord is the beginning of wisdom and the source of blessing.
2) Lord, teach us to carefully respect you, your Word, your Church and others, that the life of Christ within us may have a powerful impact on our society.
3) Enable us to live out the two great commandments – to love you and to love others – that our relationship with you may fill our hearts with joy to overflowing.
4) Lord, may our close walk with you bring us favour with all those we meet or come into contact with, in any and every situation.
5) Lord, may we live our lives with our confidence in you, and not be afraid of what others may think of us or do to us.

12th Joshua 2:10-16
Testimonies of God's deeds

1. Thank you for our testimonies of the grace of God in our lives, and especially for our salvation in Christ Jesus.
2. Lord, whenever we feel doubtful or our faith is weak, bring to our remembrance all that you have done for us in the past, that we may have faith for our present situations.
3. Teach us to be people who, in everything, see the hand of God, and so give you thanks, for this is your will, O God.
4. May we boast, not in our own achievements, but in all that you have done for us, and especially for the cross of Christ, where we find eternal life.
5. Give us the opportunities and the courage to share with non-believers every answer to prayer, that they may know the power, love and working of our God.

13th Joshua 2:17-24 (1)
Keeping our word

1) Lord, teach us to remember that you expect us to be people who do not break our promises, but always keep our word.
2) Holy Spirit, please reveal to us any aspect of our characters where we lack integrity, and help us to change.
3) Keep us from fickle-mindedness, O Lord, so that our "Yes" always means "Yes" and our "No" means "No".
4) Let no lie, half-truth or words of deception cross the lips of those who call you 'Lord'.
5) As you will never break your covenant of grace with us, may we become like you: people who keep our promises, no matter what the cost may be.

 Joshua 2:17-24 (2)
The scarlet cord

1) Thank you, Lord, for the 'scarlet cord' that runs through the whole of the Bible, prophetically pointing to the sacrifice of the coming Christ.
2) Thank you for the sacrifice of Abel's lamb in Genesis 4:4 that first prophetically indicated the need for the sacrificial Lamb to die in our place.
3) Thank you for the blood of the Passover lamb that prophetically points us to the blood of the Lamb of God, whose blood would be shed for our sins.
4) Thank you for the prophetic picture in Isaiah 53:7 of Jesus, the Lamb of God, willingly dying in our place.
5) Thank you for the prophetic picture of the risen Lamb of God in all his heavenly glory in Revelation 5:6; Lord, teach us to be a thankful, worshipful people.

 Joshua 3:1-5
Consecrate yourselves

1) Lord, you have said, 'Be holy, for I am holy'. Bring to our minds and cause us to be separate from anything that is displeasing to you.
2) Teach us how to live in the world, as salt and light, and yet to be separate from it.
3) Lord, we now re-consecrate our bodies to you; may we live only as befits a living temple of the living God.
4) Lord, we now re-consecrate our minds to you; may our thoughts be worthy of you.
5) Lord, we now re-consecrate our whole lives to you; guide us in your paths; lead us into your purposes, and use us for your glory.

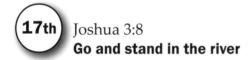

16th Joshua 3:6-7
Follow the Ark

1. As the Ark contained the Ten Commandments, help us to be careful to follow your commands.
2. Lord, help us always to keep our eyes focused on you as our first priority, and not to allow ourselves to be distracted at any time.
3. Where you lead us, O Lord, may we have the courage and determination to follow.
4. May we read and act upon your Word, so that it is a lamp to our feet and a light for our path.
5. Enlighten us as we meditate upon your Word, that we may receive your divine wisdom, which will cause us to prosper in all areas of our lives.

17th Joshua 3:8
Go and stand in the river

1. Give us the courage, O God, to step out in faith whenever necessary and 'get our feet wet'.
2. Lord, I believe; help my unbelief!
3. Teach us the difference between presumption and faith, and the wisdom to hold back when it is presumption, and to step out when it is faith.
4. Help us to keep our eyes not on problems that could flood over us, but on the Creator of the waters in the flood.
5. Lord, when you tell us to "Go!" may we not fail you by doing nothing through fear.

18th Joshua 3:9-13
Victory over enemies

1. Lord, help us to realise the authority we have as children of the living God, who have Christ living within us.

2. May the God of peace soon crush satan under our feet.
3. For those of us who may be under a spiritual attack from the powers of darkness at this time, give them understanding and wisdom to overcome.
4. When we need to wrestle against principalities and powers, strengthen us to prevail in prayer on every occasion.
5. Rise up, O Lord, and let your enemies be scattered once again!

 Joshua 3:14-17
The step of faith

1. Lord, soften our hardened hearts, that we may have faith to see you work miracles in our lives.
2. Move in a miraculous way to stop the floodtide of evil that is sweeping our land.
3. Release the full measure of the gifts of your Holy Spirit in the midst of your Church, O God.
4. Raise up men and women with the faith and confidence to move in the gifts of words of wisdom, knowledge, faith, healing, miracles, prophecy, discernment of spirits, tongues and interpretation.
5. Lord, let your Church once again be a church where the miraculous is commonplace – that you may receive all the glory.

 Joshua 4:1-7
A memorial of God's work

1. Lord, may we never forget your wondrous work of grace on the cross, through which we have our sins forgiven.
2. Let all believers amongst us, who have not been baptised in water, be moved to do so as an outward public sign of what you have done within – for your glory.
3. Lord, let us not neglect the meeting of ourselves together, and celebrating our oneness in Christ around the communion table.

4. Give each Christian parent the grace to teach their children the ways of God through word and, above all, through example.
5. May our lives be open, living letters in which others can see and read of the presence of the living God.

21st Joshua 4:8-14
The Lord exalted Joshua

1. Lord, teach us your ways, and especially the pathway of humility.
2. Take from us every inclination to exalt ourselves, which is the product of pride, but give us the desire only to see you glorified.
3. Cause us to remember that as we humble ourselves before you, you are the One who will lift us up.
4. Forbid it, Lord, that we should boast, save in the cross of Christ, our Lord.
5. Lord, when we do well, may we do so with only the desire to hear your words, "Well done, good and faithful servant".

22nd Joshua 4:15-24
That you might always fear the Lord your God

1. Give us a righteous fear of your great holiness, not to make us afraid, but that we might have deep respect for who you are.
2. Teach us to constantly remember all your mighty acts in our lives, that we may never forget that you are a God who will never leave us nor forsake us.
3. May the memories of what you have done for us in the past give us present hope and strength for the current miracles we need in our lives.
4. Keep us from backsliding, Lord, even for a moment.
5. May the fear of God cause us never to be intimidated by the fear of man.

 Joshua 5:1-12
Circumcise...again

1. Lord, cause us to be a people of circumcised hearts – ones that submit fully to the terms of the New Covenant in Christ.
2. Lord, forgive us when we fail to obey your will, and when you have to remind us again to do what is right in your eyes.
3. May we so walk in obedience to you, that we can receive all the spiritual fruits of the Promised Land in Christ.
4. Holy Spirit, continue to convict us of any unconfessed sin in our lives that would hinder God's blessing, and we bring it to you now.
5. Lord, help us to learn from our mistakes, so that we do not end up repeating them.

 Joshua 5:13-15
Holy ground

1. Lord Jesus, we thank you that you are the Commander of the Army of the Lord, with its countless legions of angels; why, O Lord, do we fear? Forgive us, we pray.
2. Where you are is holy ground; may we remember that at all times we are in your presence and in your company.
3. Since our bodies are also temples of your Spirit, and therefore holy unto you, may we honour you with our bodies.
4. Thank you for your love that enables us to have intimacy with you, but teach us also to revere your holy Name.
5. What message, O Lord, do you have for your servants? Give us ears to hear and minds to understand your Word to us today.

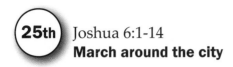

25th Joshua 6:1-14
March around the city

1. O God, when we do not understand your ways, help us never to forget that the foolishness of God is always far wiser than the wisdom of men.
2. May we never be ashamed of being a fool for Christ.
3. Reveal to us your divine strategies that will enable us to thwart any and every attack from the powers of darkness.
4. Reveal to us your divine strategies that will enable us as individuals and as churches to extend your Kingdom and build your Church.
5. Lord, when your will requires us to be silent, help us to hold our tongue.

26th Joshua 6:15-27
Overcoming the enemy

1. Lord, teach us to follow carefully all your instructions for our lives, so the devil may not have a foothold, and so we may live victoriously over all the temptations of the powers of darkness and of our carnal natures.
2. Cause us to hide in you, as our strong tower, so that our carnal ways may not get in the way of what you want to do through us.
3. We remember that your thoughts are not our thoughts, neither are your ways our ways. Help us to always do things your way.
4. Give us the boldness never to be intimidated by the enemies of God, whether humans or spirits, but rather to take our stand for righteousness.
5. Give us a big vision of what you can do through your people, and the faith, determination and perseverance to see you achieve great things for you through us.

 Joshua 7:1-13
Israel has sinned

1. Lord, show us and teach us the seriousness of sin as seen through your eyes, that we may hate sin as you hate sin.
2. Cause us to understand the destructive nature of sin – in our lives, in the life of the Church, and in the life of our nation – that we may flee from it and intercede for our nation.
3. As we grow and mature in grace, may you fine-tune our consciences, so that we may always live according to your perfect principles.
4. Reveal any sin to us and to the Church that is a cause of bringing us defeat, that we may face it, deal with it, and put it behind us.
5. May we tremble at your Word, O Lord, and hate sin as you hate sin.

 Joshua 7:14-26
The Lord turned from his fierce anger

1. As we remember that you are a God of holiness as well as a God of love, have mercy on the sins of your Church.
2. Before it is too late, have mercy on the sins of our nation that seems to delight in spurning your commandments.
3. As we remember that there is a Day of Judgment, help us to share the good news of your mercy and grace while the opportunity remains.
4. May we be able to say with the apostle Paul, "Since we know what it is to fear the Lord, we try to persuade men."
5. Lord, use us to lead others to your mercy and love in Christ, so that they may know you as Father and not as Judge.

Joshua 8:30-35
Reading God's Word

1. Lord, since your Word teaches us that there is blessing in obeying you, and the withdrawal of blessing in disobeying you, help us to be obedient in all we do.
2. Impress on us daily the importance of reading your Word, that we may constantly be reminding ourselves of your will for our lives.
3. May we be people who are able to impress your ways upon our children, by talking and by being Christlike in the home, or wherever we may be.
4. We pray for all our governors, in the local and national governments, and pray that they would return once again to the principles in your Word.
5. Enable us to have the self-discipline to read your Word regularly and systematically, so that it may nourish our souls and lives in increasing measure.

March

The Church in Action

Extracts from the Book of Acts

In the Book of Acts, we can see a number of things about the ordinary Christians in the early Church that are just as applicable to us today:

1. Jesus has commissioned his Church to carry on the ministry that he had begun, and has told us we would do the same things as he did.

2. He does not expect us to do it alone; he has given us his Holy Spirit to baptise us with power to be effective witnesses for Christ. He took the disciples from their failure, when living only in their own strength, to being very different people, when working in the strength of the Holy Spirit.

3. All the Church can be involved, since Jesus has commissioned the whole Church to serve him in this way; each has a part to play, and each has a unique contribution to make to the building of the Kingdom of God.

Each has a unique contribution to make to the building of the Kingdom of God

4. He wants us to move in the power of the Holy Spirit, so that he can achieve his plan to build his Church. This includes all the gifts of the Holy Spirit being distributed amongst his Church.

... healings and miracles occur wherever God's people happen to be ...

5. It should be normal to share our faith on a continuous basis. We see the early Church members speaking to friends and neighbours, talking to people on the streets. As they share the Good News of Jesus, healings and miracles occur wherever God's people happen to be, as the Church takes the message out everywhere.

6. The presence of God amongst them is a source of great excitement; no-one knows what God may do next, and that excitement is infectious as others catch it also. Following and serving Jesus should be an exciting adventure if we truly are in right relationship with him.

7. Spreading the Gospel is not always easy, and opposition may come in various forms - both human and spiritual sources. However, Christ has triumphed over every enemy, and so he will continue to build his Church and the gates of hell will not prevail against it. But the joy of knowing and serving Jesus can outweigh any adverse circumstance that may come against us.

As we pray through the prayer points for this month, the emphasis is on evangelism with signs and wonders during our times of outreach, that will cause many to be brought into his Kingdom. For this reason our last prayer point each day this month reiterates this heartfelt cry to God, so it may remain a priority at the forefront of our thinking and passion.

•••••••••••••••••••

1st Acts 1:1-8
Commissioned and anointed by the Holy Spirit (1)

1. Teach us to wait upon you daily, Holy Spirit, so that we always move by your guidance and in your power.
2. Give us divine strategies for witnessing and evangelism, so that we may be fruitful in our outreach, O Lord.
3. We pray for a new infilling of your Holy Spirit today; fill us afresh, and may that infilling overflow and touch the lives of others we meet today.
4. Fill us with your power to be effective witnesses for Jesus to those we meet today, O Lord, we pray.
5. Lord, we pray for our acts of witnessing and evangelism today, that you will cause many people to be convicted of sin, saved, healed and their lives completely changed as they hear the Gospel and meet with Jesus.

2nd Acts 1:1-8
Commissioned and anointed by the Holy Spirit (2)

1. Holy Spirit, we pray that we may allow you to change us, so that we can be powerful instruments for you to use.
2. For all in the church who have not yet received the baptism in the Holy Spirit, as they ask and seek, let the door be opened to them, we pray.
3. Help us to always understand the vital importance of seeking the help of the Holy Spirit in our service for Jesus, we pray.
4. Do a new work in our lives from this day onward, O Lord, as we allow ourselves to be changed by the Holy Spirit.
5. Lord, we pray for our acts of witnessing and evangelism today, that you will cause many people to be convicted of sin, saved, healed and their lives completely changed as they hear the Gospel and meet with Jesus.

3rd   Acts 2:1-13
Witnessing in power (1)

1. Give us a renewed baptism in power, O Lord, that will give us the boldness to do things for God that we have never done before.
2. Breathe upon your Church, O Lord, and bring a fresh breath of your presence into our midst that transforms us.
3. Radically change us, O Lord, that we may never be complacent, but have a sense of urgency to see your Kingdom grow.
4. Move amongst us in unusual ways, O God, with signs, wonders and miracles that cause the unsaved to know there is a God, and give their lives to Christ.
5. Lord, we pray for our acts of witnessing and evangelism today, that you will cause many people to be convicted of sin, saved, healed and their lives completely changed as they hear the Gospel and meet with Jesus.

4th   Acts 2:1-13
Witnessing in power (2)

1. We ask that you would distribute your spiritual gifts amongst your Church, Holy Spirit, so that your grace may be demonstrated to those who do not know you.
2. Lord, let many of us move in the gifts of speaking in tongues, prophecy and interpretation of tongues.
3. Lord, let many of us move in the gifts of healings, miracles and faith, to be effective in evangelism.
4. Lord, let many of us move in the gifts of discerning of spirits, words of knowledge and words of wisdom, to be effective in evangelism.
5. Lord, we pray for our acts of witnessing and evangelism today, that you will cause many people to be convicted of sin, saved, healed and their lives completely changed as they hear the Gospel and meet with Jesus.

 Acts 2:22-28
Preaching Jesus

1. Lord, give us opportunities to share with someone about Jesus today.
2. Help us, O Lord, to be able to always share the Good News about Christ, in a clear and simple way so all can understand.
3. Keep our vision focused on the cross, O God, so that we may be motivated to reach the lost.
4. As we remember the cross, and the grace we have been shown that enabled our sins to be forgiven, give us a passion to see others share in the blessings of salvation, we pray.
5. Lord, we pray for our acts of witnessing and evangelism today, that you will cause many people to be convicted of sin, saved, healed and their lives completely changed as they hear the Gospel and meet with Jesus.

 Acts 2:29-35
The resurrection

1. Lord, may we know you more and the power of your resurrection in our lives.
2. As we look forward to a life lived with you in eternity, O Lord, motivate us to bring this great hope to those who are as yet unsaved, we pray.
3. We pray for all those of your people who are struggling in their spiritual lives at the moment; give them a renewed vision of the resurrection and eternal life.
4. Cause us always to remember, O Lord, that by your death and resurrection you have triumphed over sin, death and the powers of darkness, and so be encouraged.
5. Lord, we pray for our acts of witnessing and evangelism today, that you will cause many people to be convicted of sin, saved, healed and their lives completely changed as they hear the Gospel and meet with Jesus.

7th Acts 2:36-41
Conviction and repentance

1. We pray that we will see such a response to the sharing of the Gospel that many will be 'cut to the heart' and repent.
2. May your presence be so heavy in our meetings, O God, that no sinner could fail to respond to the convicting power of the Holy Spirit.
3. We pray for your presence in our midst to be so evident that there will come a conviction of sin, even before the preaching of your Word.
4. Let us see many people crying out to God for forgiveness, and then being born again.
5. Lord, we pray for our acts of witnessing and evangelism today, that you will cause many people to be convicted of sin, saved, healed and their lives completely changed as they hear the Gospel and meet with Jesus.

8th Acts 2:42-47
God in the midst

1. Come and dwell amongst your people in a demonstrably obvious way, O Lord.
2. May we never have 'just another meeting', O Lord, but may each one be a fresh encounter with the living God.
3. May our church be known as a place where the very presence of God is, and where people can start a new life.
4. Lord, help us surrender all to you, so that you may have your way completely amongst us.
5. Lord, we pray for our acts of witnessing and evangelism today, that you will cause many people to be convicted of sin, saved, healed and their lives completely changed as they hear the Gospel and meet with Jesus.

9th Acts 3:1-9
Evangelism and the gifts of the Spirit

1. Holy Spirit, enable us to be sensitive to you, and to be able to use the gifts of the Spirit in situations outside the church building.
2. Lord, let us see more healings on the streets and in the workplaces and homes as we step out in faith.
3. Lord, cause us to be able to use healings and miracles as opportunities to share the Gospel of Christ.
4. May we bring glory to you, Lord Jesus, by acting in faith and not just by sight and, in so doing, see you save people through us.
5. Lord, we pray for our acts of witnessing and evangelism today, that you will cause many people to be convicted of sin, saved, healed and their lives completely changed as they hear the Gospel and meet with Jesus.

10th Acts 5:12-16
Miracles, signs and wonders

1. Lord, may we be the people of power that you desire us to be.
2. Lord, help us to use the power and authority, that you have delegated to us, to be a people who move naturally in miracles, signs and wonders.
3. Lord, we pray that miracles in our meetings will become the normal occurrence.
4. Lord, we pray that miracles in all places outside our meetings will become commonplace, and that we will share many testimonies as a result.
5. Lord, we pray for our acts of witnessing and evangelism today, that you will cause many people to be convicted of sin, saved, healed and their lives completely changed as they hear the Gospel and meet with Jesus.

 **Acts 8:1-7**
Evangelism

1. Lord, as we evangelise, help us to overcome all opposition from the powers of darkness.
2. Lord, raise up many evangelists from amongst us, who will lead many to Christ.
3. We pray that your Holy Spirit will be moving so strongly on those we witness to, that they will all pay close attention to our message.
4. Let us be a people who are like those who "preached the Word wherever they went".
5. Lord, we pray for our acts of witnessing and evangelism today, that you will cause many people to be convicted of sin, saved, healed and their lives completely changed as they hear the Gospel and meet with Jesus.

 Acts 8:8-13
Saved from the kingdom of darkness

1. We pray that we will see many, who are engaged in the occult, turn to Christ and be saved.
2. Lord, may unbelievers be astonished by what they see in us, your people.
3. Enable us to see many, who are currently in spiritual bondage, set free by the power of Christ.
4. Let us see many people being baptised in water in the coming days, O Lord, as they give their lives to Christ.
5. Lord, we pray for our acts of witnessing and evangelism today, that you will cause many people to be convicted of sin, saved, healed and their lives completely changed as they hear the Gospel and meet with Jesus.

13th Acts 8:14-17
The Holy Spirit

1. May we not only see many saved, O God, but also baptised in the Holy Spirit.
2. May we also be a people who allow the Holy Spirit to change us, so that daily we grow more and more like Jesus.
3. Inspire us daily, Holy Spirit, that we may know the mind of God for our daily lives.
4. Lord, let us move in the plans and purposes you have for our lives, daily.
5. Lord, we pray for our acts of witnessing and evangelism today, that you will cause many people to be convicted of sin, saved, healed and their lives completely changed as they hear the Gospel and meet with Jesus.

14th Acts 8:18-25
Spiritual discernment

1. Lord, give us spiritual discernment to see things as you see them.
2. Help us, Lord, to discern the true thoughts and hearts of men and women, and may that enable us to witness to them more effectively.
3. May we never be ignorant of the plans and strategies of the powers of darkness, O God.
4. Lord, help us to be "as wise as serpents and as harmless as doves".
5. Lord, we pray for our acts of witnessing and evangelism today, that you will cause many people to be convicted of sin, saved, healed and their lives completely changed as they hear the Gospel and meet with Jesus.

Acts 8:26-29
Divine appointments

1. Lead us to those you want us to witness to, Holy Spirit, we ask.
2. Help us to recognise your voice, O Lord, and distinguish it from our own thoughts.
3. Help us to know your prompting, Holy Spirit, and be quick to act upon it, even if it seems strange or unusual.
4. Speak to us, Lord, for we, your servants, are listening.
5. Lord, we pray for our acts of witnessing and evangelism today, that you will cause many people to be convicted of sin, saved, healed and their lives completely changed as they hear the Gospel and meet with Jesus.

 Acts 8:30-40
Effective witnessing

1. Help us to become so familiar with your Word, that we can always use it effectively.
2. Give us the wisdom we need to speak to each person about Christ in a way they will understand.
3. Give us opportunities to witness to people in key places and in positions of influence.
4. Give us the joy of leading others to Christ, we pray.
5. Lord, we pray for our acts of witnessing and evangelism today, that you will cause many people to be convicted of sin, saved, healed and their lives completely changed as they hear the Gospel and meet with Jesus.

17th Acts 11:19-21
More effective witnessing

1. Let us be a people who 'gossip the Gospel' wherever we go, O Lord.

2. Help us to be effective in leading people to Christ from all countries and ethnic backgrounds.
3. Lord, may your hand be upon us in power as we serve you.
4. Lord, may we have the same experience as those who saw that "a great number of people believed and turned to the Lord".
5. Lord, we pray for our acts of witnessing and evangelism today, that you will cause many people to be convicted of sin, saved, healed and their lives completely changed as they hear the Gospel and meet with Jesus.

 Acts 11:22-26
Establishing churches

1. Build your Church in our neighbourhood, Lord Jesus, and let not the gates of hell prevail against it.
2. Lord, help us to establish Discipleship Cell groups in all key areas.
3. Lord, help us to become a church that plants many daughter churches in strategic places.
4. Raise up from within us many leaders released to lead your people in Discipleship Cell groups and church plants, we pray.
5. Lord, we pray for our acts of witnessing and evangelism today, that you will cause many people to be convicted of sin, saved, healed and their lives completely changed as they hear the Gospel and meet with Jesus.

 Acts 13:1-3
Hearing from God

1. Holy Spirit, give us the desire to wait patiently in your presence in order to hear your voice.
2. As we worship together, move among us, Holy Spirit, and reveal more of your plans for us.
3. Lord, give us open ears to hear what the Spirit is saying to the churches.

4. Let each of us know your voice, your will and your purposes for our lives.
5. Lord, we pray for our acts of witnessing and evangelism today, that you will cause many people to be convicted of sin, saved, healed and their lives completely changed as they hear the Gospel and meet with Jesus.

20th Acts 13:4-12
Overcoming spiritual opposition

1. We take authority right now over every power of darkness that would seek to stop a move of God in our church, and rebuke them now in Jesus' Name.
2. We break the power of any negative words or curses spoken over any member of the church in Jesus' Name.
3. We break the power of any negative words or curses spoken over the church in the Name of Jesus, and pray for a continuous breakthrough.
4. Rise up, O Lord, and let every spiritual power and enemy be thrown down and scattered.
5. Lord, we pray for our acts of witnessing and evangelism today, that you will cause many people to be convicted of sin, saved, healed and their lives completely changed as they hear the Gospel and meet with Jesus.

21st Acts 16:1-10
Led by the Spirit

1. Holy Spirit, show us when to speak, but also when you want us to be silent.
2. Help us to be sensitive to your will, O Lord, when it is not the same as our desires at that time.
3. Speak to us in dreams and visions, O Lord, and give us the wisdom to understand what you are saying to us.

4. Lead us today, Holy Spirit, and show us what you would have us to do and to say.
5. Lord, we pray for our acts of witnessing and evangelism today, that you will cause many people to be convicted of sin, saved, healed and their lives completely changed as they hear the Gospel and meet with Jesus.

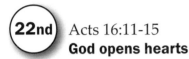

22nd Acts 16:11-15
God opens hearts

1. Holy Spirit, open the hearts of all those we witness to, so they may understand the Gospel and respond, we pray.
2. When we invite unbelievers to our Discipleship Cells, may their hearts be opened to receive the Gospel.
3. Holy Spirit, in our meetings, as the people listen to the preaching of God's Word, cause their hearts to be opened and be saved, we pray.
4. Lord, lead us to those whose hearts you will open when we speak to them, that our evangelism may be fruitful.
5. Lord, we pray for our acts of witnessing and evangelism today, that you will cause many people to be convicted of sin, saved, healed and their lives completely changed as they hear the Gospel and meet with Jesus.

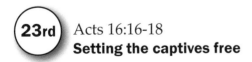

23rd Acts 16:16-18
Setting the captives free

1. We pray for those who need deliverance; give them an understanding of their need to turn to Christ.
2. For all those in our midst, who still have connections with the occult, bring a great conviction upon them, and cause them to renounce such practices completely.

3. We pray for all those in the Deliverance Team ministry, that you would enable them to minister in great power to see the captives set free.

4. We pray for all those we know whose religion is, in reality, the worship of demons; set them free by the power of the Gospel and the Name of Jesus.

5. Lord, we pray for our acts of witnessing and evangelism today, that you will cause many people to be convicted of sin, saved, healed and their lives completely changed as they hear the Gospel and meet with Jesus.

 Acts 16:19-24
Coping with trials

1. Lord, you never promised us an easy life; give us strength when in a time of trial.

2. Give us your peace, O Lord, which passes all understanding, even when our situations are tough.

3. Lord, give us the wisdom to realise that the more we seek to serve you, the more the enemy would seek to oppose us, but that "the One who is in us is greater than the one who is in the world".

4. Lord, cause us to remember that we are safe in your hands, and that nothing can happen to us outside your control.

5. Lord, we pray for our acts of witnessing and evangelism today, that you will cause many people to be convicted of sin, saved, healed and their lives completely changed as they hear the Gospel and meet with Jesus.

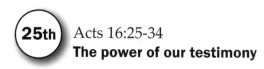 Acts 16:25-34
The power of our testimony

1. May our relationship with you be so close, O Lord, that we can rejoice in you always.

2. May the power of our praise and worship be so great, that it can cause bad situations to be turned around for good.
3. Anoint our praise and worship, O Lord, so that it becomes a mighty, spiritual weapon of warfare that defeats our spiritual enemies.
4. When people see how we react to adverse circumstances, may our testimony cause them to see the reality of Jesus in us, and desire to know him also.
5. Lord, we pray for our acts of witnessing and evangelism today, that you will cause many people to be convicted of sin, saved, healed and their lives completely changed as they hear the Gospel and meet with Jesus.

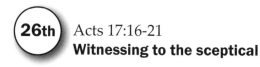 Acts 17:16-21
Witnessing to the sceptical

1. Give us patience with those who are sceptical about our message, we pray.
2. Help our faith not to be undermined by the arguments of unbelievers.
3. Give us words of wisdom when we are witnessing to sceptics, so that they can see the folly of rejecting their Creator and Saviour.
4. We pray for all those we know, whose intellect gets in the way of their knowing God; open their eyes, O Lord.
5. Lord, we pray for our acts of witnessing and evangelism today, that you will cause many people to be convicted of sin, saved, healed and their lives completely changed as they hear the Gospel and meet with Jesus.

 Acts 17:22-34
Wisdom to relate to those we speak to

1. Help us to find interesting and exciting ways to share the Gospel, O Lord.

2. Give us insight as to how to share the Gospel with those who know little of the Bible, so that we can be effective, O God.
3. Give us wisdom and clarity of thought to be able to share the Gospel with those of other faiths, and to lead them to Christ, we pray.
4. Let our very lives be living testimonies to the reality of the Lord, so that our lifestyles are powerful witnesses by themselves.
5. Lord, we pray for our acts of witnessing and evangelism today, that you will cause many people to be convicted of sin, saved, healed and their lives completely changed as they hear the Gospel and meet with Jesus.

 **28th** Acts 18:1-6
Handling opposition

1. Give us grace, we pray, when people become abusive to us just because we live for the Lord.
2. We pray for those we know, who have rejected the message of the Gospel we have shared with them; bring them to the place of understanding and repentance, O Lord.
3. Give us the wisdom to know when to remain silent in the face of opposition, O God.
4. Give us favour, O Lord, with those who have consistently rejected the Good News when we have shared it with them, and touch their hearts to change their minds.
5. Lord, we pray for our acts of witnessing and evangelism today, that you will cause many people to be convicted of sin, saved, healed and their lives completely changed as they hear the Gospel and meet with Jesus.

 29th Acts 18:7-11
Invisible assistance

1. Thank you, Lord, that you said you will never leave us nor forsake us; in all situations, help us never to forget those words.

2. Cause us to remember that those who are with us are more than those who are with the enemy.
3. Lord, keep us from being afraid to witness, since we know that you are with us.
4. As we pray, O Lord, may you release your warrior angels to win each spiritual battle in the heavenly realms.
5. Lord, we pray for our acts of witnessing and evangelism today, that you will cause many people to be convicted of sin, saved, healed and their lives completely changed as they hear the Gospel and meet with Jesus.

 30th Acts 18:18-26
Learning to become more effective

1. Give us humble spirits, O Lord, so that we remain teachable and open to instruction.
2. Help us to recognise those areas of weakness in our lives, and learn to grow stronger and wiser in those areas.
3. Holy Spirit, show us how we can learn to be more effective servants of the Lord, and give us the grace to spend time in learning how to do so.
4. Show us our gifts and callings, Holy Spirit, and help us to become more and more fruitful as we serve you.
5. Lord, we pray for our acts of witnessing and evangelism today, that you will cause many people to be convicted of sin, saved, healed and their lives completely changed as they hear the Gospel and meet with Jesus.

 31st Acts 18:27-28
Using the Scriptures effectively

1. Lord, help us not to become so busy that we neglect our times of waiting on you and reading your Word, which is our necessary spiritual food.

2. Help us, O Lord, to know your Word and become powerful in our use of it.
3. Lord, give us the wisdom to be able to use your Word as a sharp double-edged sword that penetrates even to dividing soul and spirit, and bringing conviction of sin to those we witness to.
4. Lord, cause us to be like skilled workmen, who correctly handle the Word of Truth.
5. Lord, we pray for our acts of witnessing and evangelism today, that you will cause many people to be convicted of sin, saved, healed and their lives completely changed as they hear the Gospel and meet with Jesus.

April

Practical Christian Living
James Chapters 1 to 5

This month, we are praying through a book in the New Testament that deals with the practicalities of living out the Christian life. James was one of the children of Joseph and Mary, and therefore a half-brother of Jesus. He came to believe in Jesus as the Son of God after the resurrection, and went on to become the well-respected leader of the church in Jerusalem.

Whereas Paul, as the apostle to the Gentiles, focused in his letters on how we are saved by faith in Christ alone, James takes up the situation after a person has accepted Christ by faith, and then shows how, if it is a genuine faith, it will manifest itself in a practical way as the love of Christ starts to shine out through the believer. We are not saved by doing good works, but we are saved in order to do good works. For James, if a person knows Christ, then the light of Christ must shine out in a person's practical life. And if the fruit of the new life in Christ cannot be seen, then, although that person may profess a relationship with God, in reality there is no evidence that they are really saved at all.

> **We are not saved by doing good works, but ... in order to do good works**

| ... the words that we use ... are merely a product of what is truly happening in our heart | James' book is very practical in nature. It deals with attitudes towards other people; the new birth requires a radical, new way of life, and a completely different way of looking at people than the world does. It deals with the words that we use, since they are merely a product of what is truly happening in our heart. It deals with actions, which are a reflection to what degree we have been changed from within. It deals with how we treat other people. It deals with our prayer life. And running through the letter is the need to bear up under trials, which are a means of developing our character spiritually. |

As we pray through this book, it will challenge us on all these practical areas of the Christian life, and enable us to become more practically effective in our Christian lives and ministries.

• • • • • • • • • • • • • • • • • •

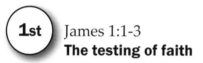

1st James 1:1-3
The testing of faith

1. Lord, we know that trials can enable us to grow; help us to grow spiritually whenever we have trials, we pray.
2. Help us to view trials in a positive way that increases our faith, and not in a negative way that saps our faith, we pray.
3. Give us a perseverance in times of trial, O Lord, that enables us to overcome all circumstances.
4. Cause us to remember that the Christian life is a marathon and not a sprint, and help us to keep our eyes always on the finishing line.
5. Lord, we pray for all we know at present who are struggling in times of trial; give them strength and encouragement to persevere.

2nd James 1:4
Becoming mature

1. Lord, help us to grow up in our spiritual lives, and not remain infants indefinitely.
2. Holy Spirit, help us to become mature in our character, daily developing further the fruit of the Spirit and the character of Christ.
3. Help us to become mature in our dealings with others, O God, that we may become spiritual fathers and mothers of those younger in the faith.
4. Help us to become mature in our relationship with you, O Lord, learning more how to have the mind of Christ and acting accordingly.
5. Help us to become mature, O God, in all our service for you, learning how to give into your Kingdom and not just to receive.

3rd James 1:5
Wisdom

1. Give us wisdom in all our affairs at work, school or college, O Lord.
2. Give us wisdom in all our dealings with one another in the church, O God.
3. Give us wisdom in all our domestic and family affairs, O Lord, that we may always live according to your Word.
4. Give us wisdom as we read your Word, O God; speak to us through your Word, and help us to learn more of you day by day.
5. Give us wisdom in the way we speak throughout the day - at home, at work, in our neighbourhoods and in church - always seasoning our conversations with divine grace.

4th James 1:6-8
Believe without doubting

1. Lord, we believe; help us in our times of doubt to rise above every situation and to trust your Word totally.
2. Guide us in our prayers, O Lord, so that when we pray we can see mountains moved.
3. We pray, O Lord, for all those unsaved people we know and are praying for; save them now, we ask.
4. Holy Spirit, as you distribute your spiritual gifts amongst the church, cause each of us to recognise what you have given us and to use it in power.
5. We bring our nation before you, O Lord, and pray that once again you would move in revival power in every area of the nation's life.

 5th James 1:9-11
Humility

1. Lord, cause us to remember that we are what we are only because of your grace on our lives, and to thank you daily.
2. We acknowledge, O Lord, that whatever we possess is as a result of what you have enabled us to earn and receive; may we be good stewards of all our possessions, we pray.
3. Lord, our strength comes from you; give us the strength and grace we need for this day, we ask.
4. Teach us how we should put the interests of others before our own, in a way that is pleasing to you, O God.
5. Teach us to look to you for our strength, O Lord, who will always give us grace for every task and situation.

 James 1:12
Persevering

1. Let us be people who never give up when we pray.
2. We pray for those we know, who are experiencing a 'wilderness' situation at present; give them the grace to persevere in their time of trial.
3. As you looked beyond the cross, Lord Jesus, to the joy that awaited you, cause us always to be able to look beyond the time of trial, to the joy you will bring when we have come through.
4. May we always remember, O God, that your love for us remains constant, no matter how we may be feeling as a result of our circumstances, and encourage our hearts.
5. Make us strong in character, in prayer and in determination never to give up at all costs.

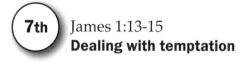 James 1:13-15
Dealing with temptation

1. Lord, give us discernment to see any likely temptation that could come our way, and thereby avoid its power.
2. Give us wisdom to make choices that ensure we do not expose ourselves to temptation, we pray.
3. Give us strength to overcome every temptation that comes our way, O Lord.
4. Forgive us, O Lord, for the times we have fallen into temptation, and give us the resolve not to repeat those failures.
5. Help us to become so familiar with your Word, O God, that whenever we are in a situation that would compromise our testimony, we can always know the right choices to make.

8th James 1:16-18
Good gifts from our Heavenly Father

1. Heavenly Father, we thank you for every good gift that we have received from your hand; cause us to be a grateful people who do not grumble.
2. Give us your grace, we pray, to deal with all people as Jesus did, no matter who they are.
3. Give us a greater measure of spiritual discernment and wisdom in all our affairs of life, we pray.
4. Create within us more and more of your love, joy, peace, patience, kindness, goodness, gentleness, faithfulness and self-control, we pray.
5. We pray for the good gift of the Holy Spirit and the gifts of the Spirit, not for our benefit alone, but that others may benefit from the gifts operating through us.

 9th James 1:19-21
Quick to listen, slow to anger

1. Make us quick to listen and slow to anger, we pray.
2. Teach us to be unselfish people, who take interest in others, as demonstrated by our willingness to listen to them.
3. Convict us, Holy Spirit, when our anger is not a righteous anger, but instead is coming from selfishness, and help us to change.
4. Give us ears that can always listen to the voice of the Holy Spirit speaking to us, we pray.
5. Help us to be angry at sin and unrighteousness, but compassionate with those who, like us, are not perfect.

James 1:22-26
Putting God's Word into action

1. Help us, O Lord, to be doers of your Word and not merely listeners, we pray.
2. You have delegated your authority to your Church to go in your Name, Lord Jesus; may we fan the flames within us to do so.
3. Give us the courage and boldness to overcome fear and to take your Word out to all the world.
4. Anoint those who regularly go out on the streets, and let them see many saved, healed and added to your Church as a result, we pray.
5. May we not be Sunday Christians only, O God, but 24-hours-a-day, 7-days-a-week, 52 weeks-a-year practisers of your Word.

 James 1:27
Caring for the needy

1. Give us hearts of compassion for those in need, we pray.
2. Give us the wisdom, and show us who in particular you would have us help financially, O Lord.
3. Bless and anoint our missionaries, who are caring for orphans and widows; may the love of Christ enable them to receive everlasting life as well as physical help.
4. Help us to always strive to remain unpolluted by the ungodly things of this world, we pray.
5. Enable us to live effectively in this world, doing all you desire of us, O Lord, changing others for Christ, without ourselves being changed by the ungodly ways of the world.

12th James 2:1-7
No favouritism

1. Teach us to love with the *agapé* love of God that chooses always to treat each person in the very best way possible.
2. Give us a heart like that of Barnabas, who was always encouraging to greater heights those whom others disregarded.
3. For those people we find very difficult to live or work with, we release them now from any feelings of unforgiveness, and pray a blessing on them now.
4. Teach us to see the value in each person, no matter who they are, and enable us to help them to their full potential, we pray.
5. We pray for all those in our midst: the rich and the poor, the well-educated and the not so well-educated, from every nation and background, and pray, "Lord, raise each of them up to their highest level of achievement in you".

13th James 2:8-11
The Royal Law

1. Holy Spirit, we ask you to continually work within us, so that our love for God grows, together with our love for people.
2. Lord, help us to hide your Word in our hearts that we may not sin against you.
3. Lord, your Word says, "Blessed are they who keep his statutes and seek him with all their heart"; may that be our experience daily, we pray.
4. O Lord, as we delight in your ways and walk in your ways; may we be like a tree planted by streams of water that yields its fruit in due season and prospers.
5. Fill us afresh this day, Holy Spirit, we pray, and may it overflow from us to touch all those with whom we come into contact today.

 James 2:12-13
Mercy

1. Since we have received your mercy, O Lord, give us merciful hearts towards others.
2. We pray for all those who have hurt us, and we now forgive and release them from our resentment.
3. We pray for all those who are unsaved, with whom we come into contact day by day; have mercy on them and save them, we pray.
4. We pray for all those who do not like us because of our walk with the Lord; have compassion on them and save them, we pray.
5. For any close relative who may have hurt us, we pray for them now, and ask you to touch their hearts and change them, O Lord.

 James 2:14-22
Faith demonstrated by actions

1. Cause us to be a people whose very actions are a sermon about the love of Christ within us.
2. May our actions always be consistent with our profession of faith in Christ, so that others have no cause to be critical of the message of the Gospel.
3. May our knowledge of salvation by faith in Christ cause us to be men and women of action, declaring our faith by all means.
4. May our faith grow to be as strong as Abraham's, so that we are able to trust your Word, O Lord, in every situation, no matter how impossible it may seem.
5. As Abraham was called 'God's friend', enable us to draw so close to you, O God, that we may share your thoughts and desires.

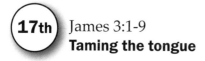 **James 2:23-26**
God's righteousness

1. Thank you, O Lord, for the righteousness with which you clothe us in Christ.
2. Thank you, O Lord, that we have been justified through our faith in Jesus, and all our unrighteousness removed by the blood of Jesus.
3. Thank you, O Lord, that you have sanctified us and set us apart for you eternally.
4. Thank you, O Lord, that because of all that Jesus has done for us, we are in the process of being glorified by you.
5. Cause us to live out our lives in a way that is worthy of the Name of Christ.

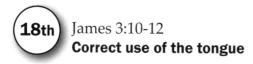 **James 3:1-9**
Taming the tongue

1. Help us to think before we speak, O Lord.
2. May we be people who use our words to build others up and not cut them down, we pray.
3. Help us to be mindful of those we speak to, so that we can know when our words would cause unnecessary injury, and so speak carefully.
4. Keep us from all forms of gossip, O Lord, for it is not an act of love.
5. May our tongues never be silent in praising and thanking you, O Lord, for all you mean to us and do for us.

18th James 3:10-12
Correct use of the tongue

1. Bless and anoint all those who teach in our Children's Ministries, we pray; may their words remain in the children's hearts.

2. Bless and anoint all those who teach our youth; may their words bring life-changing guidance and direction to our young people.
3. We pray for all the preaching in the church; Holy Spirit, guide and lead, so that your Word for that very moment may always be spoken.
4. We pray you will anoint our words as we witness to people day by day, O Lord.
5. Give each of us the ability to speak to you, O Lord, in tongues; stir up the gift if it is dormant, and provide the gift if it is not yet present.

 **James 3:13-17**
True wisdom

1. Give us the wisdom to allow you to search our hearts, O Lord, and help us remove any thought, motive or desire that is not pleasing in your sight.
2. Give us the wisdom that makes us a people who are peace-loving; for all those in the church, who are in conflict with someone, bring healing and reconciliation, O Lord.
3. Give us the wisdom to be fruitful in all areas of our lives.
4. Give us the wisdom to know which ministries you have given to us, and then make us fruitful as we diligently put them into practice.
5. Give us the wisdom in talking to people, so we may bring the unsaved to Christ; the backslider back to the Lord, and to encourage each believer to function in their maximum anointing.

 **James 3:18**
Peacemakers

1. May we be known not merely as peace*keepers* but peace*makers*, in every area of our lives, we pray.

2. As we seek to be peacemakers, O Lord, help us to raise a harvest of righteousness in our lives, and in the lives of those with whom we are in contact.
3. For those in your church who, at the present time, have, for any reason, lost their peace that comes from having a relationship with you, restore it to them now, we pray.
4. We pray for any of the families in the church that are troubled at the present time, especially with strained relationships; may the peace of God be restored to them, O Lord.
5. Help us this day to lead someone to the Lord, so that thereby they find peace with God through faith in Jesus.

 James 4:1-3
Praying with the right motives

1. Give us clean hands and a pure heart, O Lord, so that nothing contaminates effective prayer in our lives.
2. Help us to know the mind of Christ, so that we can always pray in perfect accordance with your will, O Lord.
3. Guide us, Holy Spirit, so that whatever we ask in prayer, it may not be from selfish motives, but from motives that you are pleased with.
4. If our prayer life seems ineffective, and if the cause is our motives, then enable us to understand, Holy Spirit, so we can change.
5. Remove from us any inclination to be quarrelsome, O Lord, that we may live in peace with others insofar as it depends on us.

 James 4:4-6
No friendship with the world

1. Test our hearts, O Lord, and reveal to us any love of the world that is not pleasing to you, and help us to change.
2. As we live and work in the world and serve you here, O God, give us the wisdom not to be drawn into the world's ways, but to remain untainted by its ways.

3. Help us to love the sinner, O God, but not to love sinful ways.
4. If there are any strongholds of the world already in our lives, O Lord, show us and help us to break them right now.
5. Give us the grace, O God, to shun, as your Word says, "the cravings of sinful man; the lust of the eyes, and the boasting of what he has and does".

23rd James 4:7
Resisting the devil

1. Teach us to submit to you in our thoughts, our words and our actions, O Lord.
2. Help us to ensure that the devil has no foothold in any area of our lives, we pray.
3. Enable us to put on all the spiritual armour of God, and to extinguish every flaming arrow from the evil one.
4. May our faith rise up on every occasion needed to resist the plans of the devil.
5. May no weapon formed against us be able to stand, O Lord, but give us the wisdom to know the plans of the evil one.

24th James 4:8-10
Lifted up by God

1. Teach us how to humble ourselves before you, O God, so that in due course you can lift us up.
2. Enable the attitude of Christ Jesus to be ours also, O Lord.
3. Teach us the way of servanthood and servant leadership in all areas of the church, we pray.
4. Give us the faith that enables us to trust you, so that we do not need to try and promote ourselves or our own interests, knowing that you will raise us up in due time.
5. Cause us to work out our salvation with fear and trembling, knowing that it is God who works in us to will and to act according to his good purpose.

 **James 4:11-12**
No slander

1. Keep our lips from slander, O Lord, for this belongs to the world, not the Kingdom of God.
2. Help us to protect the reputation of our brothers and sisters in Christ, even when they have let us down, we pray.
3. Help us always to see the good in each individual, rather than dwelling on the bad.
4. Cause us to remember the plank in our own eyes, O God, before we attempt to point out the speck in someone else's.
5. For those who have slandered us or spoken badly about us, we now forgive them in Jesus' Name.

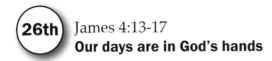 **James 4:13-17**
Our days are in God's hands

1. Teach us to number our days, O Lord, and thereby have the humility to remember that each day is a gift from God.
2. Convict us, O God, so that we do not waste our days in idleness or in fruitless activity, but rather use them profitably for God.
3. Keep our lips from boastful speech, O Lord, and may our focus be on you rather than on ourselves.
4. Keep us Christ-centred, O Lord, and not self-centred.
5. Forgive us for the sins of omission (not doing what we should be doing), as well as the sins of commission (doing what we should not do).

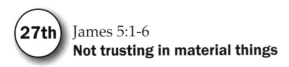 **James 5:1-6**
Not trusting in material things

1. Thank you for our material blessings, O Lord; we acknowledge that we are merely stewards of all you have given us.

2. Give us the wisdom to use our material wealth in a way that pleases you, O Lord.
3. Bless the giving of our hands, our tithes and our offerings, which we return back to you.
4. May our trust always be in you, O God, and never in only that which we can see.
5. If we are not using our material wealth as you would have us to, then, Holy Spirit, speak to our hearts and show us how to change.

 James 5:7-12
Patience

1. As we wait on you in prayer, O Lord, give us the patience to wait for your perfect timing, knowing you do all things well.
2. For those of us who have been praying for a long time for matters of concern, give us the patience to keep praying and to never give up.
3. Teach us to have the faith of Job, who never ceased to trust you, O Lord, even when he did not understand his suffering.
4. As we sometimes need to sow in tears, may we reap with songs of joy when the harvest time finally comes.
5. Cause us to remember at all times, O Lord, that your coming is near, and may we live in the light of your coming.

 James 5:13-16
Praying for the sick

1. Give each one the faith to call for prayer in times of sickness and in need, and reward each act of faith, we pray.
2. Give us the faith to pray for the sick, confidently believing that God will heal.
3. We pray for an outbreak of signs and wonders, as the church rises up in faith to exercise the spiritual gifts.

4. We pray for our teams that pray for the sick on the streets; cause them to have a greater anointing to see many healed and so turn to Christ.
5. We pray for all the elders in the church as they minister to others, give them an ever-increasing anointing to see breakthroughs in the lives of those they pray for.

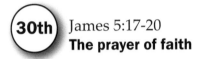

30th James 5:17-20
The prayer of faith

1. Elijah was a human being with the same emotions as we have; may we also prevail in prayer as he did.
2. Give us the faith to pull down strongholds and to see all manner of situations turned around, we pray.
3. Holy Spirit, release the gift of faith more and more into your Church, we pray.
4. Lord, we believe; help us in our times of unbelief.
5. Lord, release a faith into your Church, we pray, that will see the spiritual drought in our nation broken, and the sound of the abundance of the living waters breaking over our land.

May

Transparent Before God

Psalms 139, 112 and 15

The Book of Psalms, although being prayers, consists of a collection of five Jewish hymn books, with the psalms being set to music to be sung. They contain some of the most personal expressions of heartfelt cries to God, through a wide spectrum of feelings: from the desperate plea of one in deepest distress, on the one hand, to the high praises, on the other, of one rejoicing in everything, prospering exceedingly well in their lives.

Approximately half the 150 psalms were written by David, with the others being written by a variety of other men, who tended to be, like David, choir and worship leaders who had a prophetic gifting, writing under the inspiration of the Holy Spirit.

One of the noticeable aspects to the contents of the psalms is the transparency with which the psalmists operate before God to express their feelings. God knows everything about us before we even begin to pray, so it is a sensible policy to be completely open and honest before God. David, three of whose psalms we are praying through this month, was just like that.

> ... it is a sensible policy to be completely open and honest before God

These are times for drawing deeply on the spiritual roots within him

Sometimes he feels as though he has been praying for ever, and God does not seem to be answering. These are times for drawing deeply on the spiritual roots within him and which result, when the answer to prayer is finally seen, in a process of character building that has been taking place during those long, hard times of waiting on God. Other times, he is seeing victory after victory, during a season in his life of overcoming enemies and enjoying God's blessing.

Of the three psalms of David this month, the first is Psalm 139, which expresses the qualities that only God has. Verses 1-6 demonstrate God's omniscience – he knows all things, every detail, especially about you and me. Verses 7-12 reveal his omnipresence – he is always everywhere at the same time – so we are never alone, even if we feel it is so. Verses 13-16 show God's omnipotence – there is nothing he cannot do, so we need have no fear. With this knowledge of his Creator, David seeks to be totally transparent in his dealings with God.

Psalms 112 and 15 each indicate that those who walk honourably before God will know his blessing and security, developing a faith that cannot be shaken by outward traumas. As we pray through the prayer points this month, we are seeking to develop such a character, which enables us to be the people and ministers of God that he wants us to be to achieve his plans and purposes.

• • • • • • • • • • • • • • • • • •

1st Psalm 139:1
Search me, O Lord

1. Lord, you know every detail of our lives; reveal to us, Holy Spirit, anything within us that is not pleasing to you, so we may change.

2. If our ambitions are not in line with your will, O Lord, show us so that we can realign our lives to your will.
3. You know our hearts, O God. If we are harbouring anything there that hinders our walk with you, show us so that we may deal with it.
4. For all the things that we are doing right, strengthen and expand those areas of our lives for your glory, we pray.
5. Help us to remain transparent before you at all times, O Lord, realising that, although you know all things, you want us to seek to hide nothing from you.

2nd Psalm 139:2
Godly thoughts

1. Since our mind is the enemy's target, help us to bring all our thoughts into captivity, so that he may have no hold over us.
2. Let the meditations of our hearts be pleasing to you, O Lord.
3. If we are harbouring any thoughts of unforgiveness in our hearts, O God, help us now to resolve to release them.
4. May our thoughts be continually turning towards you, O Lord, in everything we are doing during the course of the day.
5. As we seek your face, reveal your thoughts to us today, Holy Spirit.

3rd Psalm 139:3
Godly actions

1. Lord, you know our weaknesses; give us your boldness and courage to step out in faith, even when we feel inadequate.
2. Give us divine appointments to witness to those you know are ready to be saved - on the streets, in our places of work, or wherever we happen to be.
3. Help us, where appropriate, to use the gifts of the Spirit: tongues, interpretation, prophecy, words of knowledge, wisdom and discernment, faith, healings and miracles.

4. Give us the boldness to step out in faith whenever we are praying for specific needs, whether for healing, or for any prayer request that needs a specific answer.
5. Anoint us afresh with your Holy Spirit right now, we pray; let your streams of living water flow out from our innermost being, we pray.

4th Psalm 139:4
Godly words

1. Teach us to be a people who think before we speak, so that we do not regret by speaking in haste.
2. Help us to see beyond a person's failings to the potential that is within them, and to speak words that will help them fulfil that potential.
3. Give us words that cause us to strengthen, encourage and comfort others.
4. Help us not to speak negative words over ourselves nor think negative thoughts that will hinder us rather than causing us to act in faith, we pray.
5. Holy Spirit, help us to speak words of faith that can see significant answers to prayer.

5th Psalm 139:5-6
God's presence

1. Lord, as we draw close to you each day, may we be more and more conscious of your presence around us, we pray.
2. Lord Jesus, in times of trouble, may we always remember that you have said you will never leave us nor forsake us.
3. May you be the first thought we have in the morning, and the last thought we have at night, O Lord.
4. Knowing you are always with us, teach us to speak to you at any time and about anything, as we fulfil our daily tasks and duties, O Lord.

5. Help us to be carriers of your presence, O Lord, so that our lives affect others even without us speaking.

 Psalm 139:7-8
Knowing the Holy Spirit

1. Help us each day to know you more, Holy Spirit, we pray.
2. Holy Spirit, enable us to learn how to know when you are speaking to us, so that we can obey all you desire us to do.
3. Cause us to desire to be continually filled afresh with the Holy Spirit, never allowing our light to diminish.
4. As we read the Bible, enlighten our minds to understand the depths of the things you would have us know and learn, we pray.
5. O Lord, help us to use the gifts of the Spirit in a way that brings glory to Jesus and fulfils your purposes.

 Psalm 139:9-10
Guided by the Holy Spirit

1. Teach us to be responsive to your guidance and to your leading in our lives, Holy Spirit, we pray.
2. Knowing that everything we do is important to you, guide us in all that we have to do today, Holy Spirit.
3. Guide us in all the decisions we have to make regarding our jobs and careers, we pray.
4. Guide us in all the decisions we have to make regarding our domestic and family affairs, O Lord, so that we always make the right choices.
5. Guide us, Holy Spirit, in all areas of the ministries you have called each of us to be involved in, we pray.

8th Psalm 139:11-12
Intimacy with God at all times

1. Since you have created us, brought us into being, and sustain our lives, teach us that nothing is more important than knowing you intimately, O Lord.
2. If we are feeling dry for any reason, in our times of devotions, prayer and Bible reading, help us to draw closer to you in deeper intimacy, we pray.
3. If you are being crowded out of our lives, through our being too busy, teach us to prioritise our lives correctly, O God.
4. Cause us to understand the height, depth and breadth of the love you have for each of us, O Lord, so that we may appreciate your desire to be intimate with us.
5. Help us to love you with every fibre of our being, O Lord, and to experience the love, joy and peace that follows intimacy with you.

 9th Psalm 139:13
Accountable to our Creator

1. Lord, you have created each of us; teach us to understand that we are accountable to you in all we do.
2. Teach us the fear of the Lord, which is the beginning of wisdom, we pray.
3. Forgive us our trespasses this day, as we also forgive those who have trespassed against us.
4. If we are not currently living our lives in perfect accordance with your will, show us where we have stepped outside your will, and help us to (re)align ourselves to it.
5. In all that we say, think and do, help us to give you all the praise, glory and honour that is due to you, O Lord, as the One who created us.

10th Psalm 139:14
The wonderful works of God

1. Teach us to express our thankfulness to you for giving us the gift of life, O Lord.
2. Cause us to express our gratefulness to you for enabling us to be reborn in Christ, and so to experience eternal life, O Lord.
3. Enable us to know and outwork your will for our individual lives, O Lord, so that we can rejoice in the knowledge that we are fulfilling your plan.
4. Help us to understand the magnitude of your awesome power as Creator of all, O Lord, so that our faith may be continually growing.
5. Make us continually thankful for every answer to prayer we experience that demonstrates your wonderful works in our lives and situations, O God.

 11th Psalm 139:15
Acknowledging our dependence on God

1. Lord, help us to appreciate that we depend on you for every breath that we take, so that we do not become forgetful of all you mean to us.
2. We acknowledge that you are the One who helps us create wealth; help us in our jobs and businesses, we pray.
3. May we be a people who give generously to you and to your work, O God, as one way of acknowledging our dependence on you.
4. Heavenly Father, give us this day our daily bread, we pray.
5. We live because Jesus lived and died for us, rising again from the dead; may our lives be lived as ambassadors for you, O Lord, as an acknowledgement of our utter dependence and devotion to you.

12th Psalm 139:16
Discovering God's destiny for our lives

1. You had a plan for our lives before we were even born; help each of us to wait on you to discover what that plan is, so that we do not miss our destinies.
2. Help us to make the right choices, so that we walk the pathway in life that you have laid down for us, O Lord, not turning aside through disobedience or neglect.
3. Teach us the joy of walking in your perfect ways, even when you allow things to happen to us that do not make us feel comfortable.
4. You have called each of us to different callings and ministries; give us the patience and determination to wait on you, O Lord, to discover what they are.
5. Even if we realise you have called us to walk a difficult path, O Lord, give us the courage to always pursue the destiny we feel you leading us into, we pray.

13th Psalm 139:17-18
Prioritising God's Word in our lives

1. Your Word reveals your thoughts, O God; teach us to be systematic readers of the Bible, so that we may learn your thoughts.
2. Help us to plan our daily lives, so that reading your Word is always included.
3. Enable us, Holy Spirit, to understand the words that we read each time we read the Bible.
4. Cause us to understand, believe and stand on all the promises you make to us in your Word, O Lord.
5. Bring to our remembrance, Holy Spirit, throughout the course of each day, the things we have read in the Bible, so that we can put them into practice in all we do.

 Psalm 139:19-20
Shunning evil

1. Keep our hands from evil, O Lord.
2. Keep our eyes and our minds from evil, O Lord, helping us to say "No" when necessary.
3. Give us discernment when watching television, O Lord, guarding our minds from evil.
4. Help us to make wise decisions not to go to places that would compromise our godly standards.
5. May we learn that it is better to suffer loss than to participate in activities that may bring gain but are ungodly, O Lord.

 Psalm 139:21-22
Hating sin, loving the sinner

1. Give us minds that can discern sin, even when it is subtle or seems reasonable.
2. Cause us to learn how to love the ungodly whilst hating sin.
3. As we live in a fallen world, help us to be godly influencers of others, we pray, without being influenced ourselves by the evil around us.
4. Have mercy on the unsaved people we live and work with each day; may they come to a knowledge of salvation through Christ, we pray.
5. Because we live in a fallen world, and are surrounded by the ways of the world, help us to continually live according to the values of the Kingdom of God.

 Psalm 139:23-24
Search me, O Lord

1. Search us, O God, and know our hearts, and reveal to us everything you want us to change.

2. When you test us to help us mature in Christ, O Lord, help us to pass the test, and to grow spiritually in the process, we pray.
3. If we have any anxious thoughts, O God, help us to learn to cast all our cares on you, knowing that you care for us.
4. Father, if you see any offensive ways within us, give us the grace to be able to recognise them and act accordingly, even when it requires a trusted friend to point them out.
5. Day by day, lead us into the life-changing process of becoming more like Christ, as we move towards eternity with you, O Lord.

 Psalm 112:1
A reverence for God that brings obedience

1. May the godliness, integrity and sincerity of our lives, wherever we are and whatever we do, bring praise to you, even from the people of this world, O Lord.
2. Teach us how to have a reverent fear for you, O Lord, that enables us to possess a great authority before men and before the powers of darkness.
3. Make us a people who are not reluctant to walk in the integrity of godliness, but who delight in it.
4. As we walk in obedience to you, O God, may the power of the Holy Spirit enable us to be used in all manner of ways, circumstances and miraculous happenings that bring glory to you.
5. Cause us to be a righteous people, who can pray powerful and effective prayers that see the miraculous, just as Elijah did, who was a man just like us.

 Psalm 112:2
Praying for our children

1. Help us to raise our children in the fear and respect for the Lord, we pray.

2. Guard our children against every force of evil that would seek to corrupt their minds from an early age, O God.

3. Help our children to come to know you at an early age, O Lord, so that they can grow up to be men and women full of the wisdom of God.

4. Raise up our children to become mighty in our land, O Lord, ones who can bring about radical change for good.

5. Bless and anoint in a special way all those who teach our children the Word of God, we pray.

 Psalm 112:3

Wisdom with our material possessions

1. Give us the ability to create wealth, O Lord, together with the wisdom of how to spend it.

2. Enable each of us, from the material possessions you give us - whether much or little - to learn the blessings of tithing and giving.

3. Give us all the wealth we need to carry out the plans and purposes you have for us as a church, we pray.

4. Cause us to be good stewards of all material possessions that come our way, recognising that such things are not given for our self-indulgence.

5. Enable us to be people who hold on lightly to what we own, recognising that only spiritual wealth is enduring.

 Psalm 112:4

God works all things together for good

1. Cause us to remember, O Lord, that no darkness can hide anything from your eyes; when we feel overcome by the pressures of life, lift us up, we pray.

2. Teach us the truth that you work all things together for the good of those who love you, so that we never despair when things outwardly are not going well for us.

3. Help us to learn, O Lord, that at times you will allow difficult times to come our way, as part of the process of our developing an overcoming faith.
4. For those we know who are feeling desperate, because of undesired things going on in their lives, strengthen them in the knowledge that you can turn what is meant for evil, into good.
5. Develop within us a total trust in you, O Lord, that is able to look at any adverse circumstances and see the victory you can bring over them.

21st Psalm 112:5
Generous hearts

1. Make us a generous and not a selfish people, O Lord.
2. Teach us the truth of your words, Lord Jesus, that it is more blessed to give than to receive.
3. Develop within us the joy that comes when we sacrificially give to the benefit of another person and of the work of God.
4. Cause us to experience the spiritual truth that we will reap according to how we sow, in all areas of life, including financially.
5. Cause us to be a people who are generous with our praise for others, so that they can be built up to do greater things for God.

22nd Psalm 112:6
Not shaken

1. Cause no news that may come to our ears to shake us, because we have a total confidence in you, O God.
2. Make us a people who can always see beyond bad news, to a God who is able to do all things and change every situation, we pray.
3. Help us to so develop our relationship with you, O Lord, that the peace you give us will overcome any attempt to shake our faith.

4. Build your Church amongst us, O Lord, and may we witness the fact that the gates of hell cannot overcome it.
5. When you shake the world around us, O Lord, to cause the people to turn to you, let them see your people as ones who are unshaken by events, so that they seek our help to know Christ.

 Psalm 112:7
Standing in times of trouble

1. Let the experience we have of your perfect love for us cast out all fear, O Lord.
2. When trouble is all around us, O Lord, let the world see how we stand firm in our God, and cause them to want to know more about the God who sustains us.
3. In times of financial trouble, recession and economic shaking, watch over and protect your people, O Lord, causing them instead to prosper more.
4. In times when we experience sickness, O Lord, help us to trust you to restore our health, learning whatever lessons you want to teach us in the process, we pray.
5. Teach us to see all things, not merely in present-day circumstances, but in terms of eternity, so that we can maintain a true perspective of our light and momentary troubles.

 Psalm 112:8
Overcoming

1. In all areas of ministry, help us to overcome all obstacles, hindrances and any feelings of inadequacy, O Lord, and to stand in the strength of the Lord.
2. We pray that the Holy Spirit will be so present in all our Discipleship Cells, that every person who attends will deepen their commitment and walk with the Lord.

3. Cause us to believe together, in order to overcome every attack of the enemy upon our lives, our families, our jobs, our homes and our church.

4. Give us breakthroughs, O Lord, to see those we have been praying for come to faith in Christ and be added to the church and Discipleship Cells.

5. We take authority over every spirit of unbelief that blinds the eyes of those we are praying for; help us, O Lord, to use the authority as believers that you have given us.

25th Psalm 112:9
People of influence

1. Make us a people of influence, O Lord, regarding all those we come into contact with each day.

2. Make us strong in character; in determination to do right, and in the ability to bring godly change in all areas of life.

3. As we sow our finances into evangelism and missions, cause there to be a great harvest of souls saved, communities changed, and righteousness growing.

4. In all our areas of schools, colleges, businesses and workplaces, make us a people who can push back the darkness of ungodliness, we pray.

5. May the words we speak take on an anointing from the Holy Spirit that brings a godly influence of change to the lives of others, that we could never bring about by our own abilities.

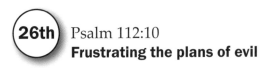

26th Psalm 112:10
Frustrating the plans of evil

1. Make us strong to the point where we can always frustrate the plans of the powers of darkness.

2. When the devil appears as an angel of light, give us discernment, so that we can see and so not be caught up in his plans.

3. When the devil comes as a roaring lion, cause us to humble ourselves before God, resist the devil, and see him flee from us, we pray.
4. Anoint our intercessory prayers, so that we can effectively oppose and frustrate every plan of the enemy.
5. As we pray, make us strong to the pulling down of every spiritual stronghold that seeks to oppose the work of God in our lives and in the church.

 Psalm 15:1
Getting closer to the Lord

1. Increase the desire in our hearts to draw closer to you, O Lord.
2. Knowing that your ways and your thoughts are so much better and higher than ours, be the Lord of our lives in everything we do.
3. Help us to shake off any slothful or lazy ways when it comes to seeking your face, O God, but instead to seek you in spirit and in truth.
4. Help us not to waste our time in a way that makes us too tired to pray, but rather to order our time daily in a way that always enables us to spend time with you.
5. Heavenly Father, teach us to learn how to love everything about you more and more, we pray.

 Psalm 15:2
Honesty and integrity

1. Cause us to be people who always speak the truth, O Lord, so that you are not dishonoured by our lack of faithfulness.
2. May we speak the truth, the whole truth, and nothing but the truth, not succumbing to telling half-truths that would cause confusion.
3. Let us be true disciples of Jesus, keeping our word, so that we let our "Yes" be "Yes" and our "No" be "No".

4. When we need to speak hard truths, help us to always be able to speak the truth in love, so that the other person is helped and not hindered.
5. May we be known amongst the unsaved as individuals who can always be trusted to be honest and sincere.

29th Psalm 15:3
Profitable words

1. Keep our lips from slander and gossip, O Lord, and may we not delight in hearing such words.
2. Keep us from angry words that are spoken in haste and regretted later; rather, help us to exercise self-control, which is a fruit of the Spirit, we pray.
3. Help us get into the habit of only ever speaking words designed to help others, not pull them down, O God.
4. Teach us to understand the power of our words, O Lord, so that we learn to use them to speak words of faith that can change people and situations for the good.
5. Teach us how to speak prayerful words of blessing over those who offend, hurt and mistreat us, knowing that this is what you have commanded us to do.

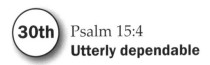

30th Psalm 15:4
Utterly dependable

1. Enable us, O Lord, to shun all forms of evil that we encounter, as we live our daily lives.
2. Teach us to honour and respect all who fear your Name, O Lord, and have given their lives to Christ, since together we form the family of God.
3. Teach us to honour and respect those who have spiritual authority over us, realising this is your will, O Lord.
4. Give us the wisdom not to make promises or enter into agreements that we cannot keep, we pray.

5. Because you are a God who never breaks his promises to us, make us a people who keep our promises, even when it hurts.

 Psalm 15:5
Unshakeable

1. Give us unshakeable faith in your Word, O God, so that we can be the people of great faith that you want us to be.
2. Help us to understand the authority you have delegated to us, Lord Jesus, so that we can overcome every evil spirit and power of darkness that opposes us.
3. As we come before you in prayer, O God, cause the power of our prayers to defeat and extinguish every fiery dart or arrow sent against us by the powers of darkness.
4. As we put on the full armour of God, when the day of evil comes, help us to stand our ground and stand firm in the mighty strength of the Lord, we pray.
5. Give us an unshakeable faith to be able to pray into existence a revival that will shake ourselves, our church, our borough, our city and our nation, O Lord.

" Save our city, O Lord, and cause a widespread revival to begin and spread out around the nation and to other nations of the world. **"**

(June 8)

June

Praying for National Repentance and Revival

Isaiah Chapters 54 to 57

Isaiah, whose name means "Yahweh is salvation", was called to the ministry during troubled times in the life of his nation. He was born into the royal family, and could have been content with a comfortable life in Jerusalem, especially as the nation was enjoying a period of prosperity not seen since the days of Solomon. And yet, he was prepared to forsake any privileges that such a position would bring him, and instead chose to obey the call of God on his life, as a prophet to preach the message of the need for national repentance. He knew that the wealth and prosperity of the nation were merely superficial. The people had turned their backs on the true God of Israel, and were shortsighted enough to believe that things would always remain as they were.

Isaiah was prepared to forsake any privileges ... and chose to obey the call of God on his life

However, because they had forsaken their God, Isaiah was commissioned by the Lord to warn the people that they needed to turn from their immorality and ungodliness in national repentance, otherwise God would remove his

Our nation is in desperate need of national repentance

favour from them, and allow them to be overrun by their enemies. This was nothing more nor less than God fulfilling the terms of the Old Covenant that the nation of Israel had agreed to years before through Moses: he would bless them if they obeyed; he would withdraw his blessing and favour if they disobeyed.

Isaiah received his famous call, recorded in Chapter 6, when he "...saw the Lord seated on a throne, high and exalted..." The vision of the Lord on his throne, surrounded by great angelic beings, had a profound effect upon him that lasted throughout his long ministry as a prophet. When hearing God ask the question, "Whom shall I send? And who will go for us?", he had no hesitation in responding with the words, "Here I am. Send me!" The reality of the contrast between the holiness of the scene in Heaven, and the ungodliness of the daily reality of life in Israel, caused him to understand the dire situation and future of the nation of Israel if they did not quickly turn in repentance.

The parallel with our own times and nation is clear. We live in times of unparalleled physical prosperity, but spiritually, as a nation, we have turned away from the truth of the true God, and are boastfully living in an ungodly fashion. God is patient but, as the Bible shows, his patience is not without limit. Our nation is in desperate need of national repentance.

Our understanding of the depravity of sin, and of the holiness of God, should evoke within each believer the urgency of the hour for our nation; the need is to intercede and to act, with our cry being, "Here I am, Lord. Send me."

• • • • • • • • • • • • • • • • • • •

1st Isaiah 54:1
The childless and spiritually childless

1. We pray for ourselves, that you would enable us, Holy Spirit, to be able to lead others to the new birth in Christ.
2. We pray for specific individuals right now, who we know are not yet saved, and ask that you will cause them to be born again through faith in Jesus.
3. Enable us, O Lord, to not only be leading others to the new birth in Christ, but to ground them in Christ, so that they are not merely converts, but disciples of Jesus.
4. We pray for our church, O God, that we will all be instrumental in bringing individuals to the new birth in Christ.
5. We pray for all those married couples we know, who are praying to be able to conceive; hear their prayers and give them children, we pray.

2nd Isaiah 54:2-3
Personal and church growth

1. Help us, O Lord, not to be content with our current spiritual situation, but to ever desire to grow deeper and wider in our relationship with you, and in the outworking of that relationship in our everyday lives.
2. We pray for our church, that the scope of its ministry may be enlarged, lengthened and widened, and that the whole assembly of your people, O Lord, will rise up in fruitful service for you.
3. Holy Spirit, help us to be prepared to leave our comfort zones, and to be willing to step out of the boat in faith, so that we can see you doing greater things through each of us.
4. Enlarge our individual ministries, O Lord, as we allow our faith to arise and to stretch, to do things for Jesus that we have never done before.
5. Give us a great harvest of souls, O God, as we continue both to pray and to be witnesses for you and, as a church, cause us to spread out in our scope of ministry and influence in our society.

 **3rd** Isaiah 54:4
Trusting in the Lord

1. Lord, give us a fresh infilling today of your Holy Spirit, so we can be bold and effective witnesses of the Gospel of Jesus Christ wherever we are.
2. Help us not to fear 'stepping out of the boat', but rather give us the courage to take each step of faith that we need to take, in order to fulfil your plans for our lives and to do your will daily.
3. Help us, O Lord, to trust you with our finances and in our giving of tithes and offerings to you.
4. Help us, O Lord, to trust you in making you the first priority in our lives, so that as we seek first the Kingdom of God, all other things will be added to us.
5. Lord, give us the boldness to seek you for, and to put into operation, the gifts of the Holy Spirit, in order that your Church may be edified, and your work amongst unbelievers extended.

 4th Isaiah 54:5
God's covenantal relationship with his people

1. Heavenly Father, help us always to remember that we are in covenantal relationship with you, just as are a husband and wife; may we always be faithful to you.
2. Help us to love you with all our being, O Lord, since what would it profit a man to gain the whole world and lose his soul?
3. You are our Maker, O God; teach us your ways, so that we may follow the Maker's instructions as set out in your Word, the Bible.
4. Lord, you love us with a holy, jealous love, not wanting us to harm ourselves by loving less worthy things; cause our love and relationship with you to deepen as each day passes.
5. Lord, you are our only Redeemer, having purchased us from sin by the blood of Jesus; help us to live, in this world, lives that are worthy of the price that has been paid to save us.

5th Isaiah 54:6-8
Restoring the sinner and backslider

1. Lord, we pray for all those we know, who may be feeling that you are no longer near them; cause them to remember that you have promised never to leave us nor forsake us. If there is sin causing the barrier, bring repentance, we ask.
2. We pray for all who once attended our church, but who have now grown spiritually cold and no longer walk with God; touch them and restore them, O God.
3. We pray for all the children of the members of our church, who are not walking with God; hear the prayers of the parents, O Lord, and bring the children into a deep relationship with you.
4. We pray for every unsaved husband of believing wives in our church; arrest them by your Holy Spirit, and bring them to salvation, we pray.
5. We pray for every unsaved wife of believing husbands in our church; arrest them by your Holy Spirit and save them, we pray.

 6th Isaiah 54:9
Like the days of Noah

1. Lord, we are living in violent days just like the days of Noah; we take authority over every spirit of violence operating in our streets, and bind them in Jesus' Name.
2. We pray for every gang member operating in and around our communities, and ask that you would cause each one to be confronted by the Gospel; respond, and be changed by the power of the Lord.
3. Lord, we live in days like Noah, when the whole world has become corrupt; have mercy on the nations of the world, and send revival in every continent, we pray.

4. Lord, as in the days of Noah, the inclination of the thoughts of the hearts of many men and women are only towards evil all the time; have mercy, and may your Church preach the life-changing Gospel of Christ, in power.

5. Who is a God like you, who pardons sin and forgives transgressions? Thank you that, if we confess our sins, you are faithful and just and will forgive our sins, and purify us from all unrighteousness.

7th Isaiah 54:10
The compassion of God

1. Lord, you are a God who justifies the sinner who comes to you for mercy; we pray that we will be able to lead many to Christ.

2. Give each of us a heart of compassion for people, just like the heart of our Heavenly Father, we pray.

3. Make us humble enough to be able to see the plank in our own eyes before criticising others for the speck in theirs.

4. Help us to love with the love of Christ, those who are considered by others as unloveable, and may that compassion help lead them to the God whose love can save them if they are willing.

5. Thank you, Lord, that because of the New Covenant in Christ's blood, each one who comes to you will never be driven away, but rather accepted by you.

8th Isaiah 54:11-12
Praying for our city

1. Have mercy on our city, O Lord, and forgive all the wickedness that is committed within its boundaries.

2. We pray for the Mayor of our city, O God, that you would cause him to make decisions that are not merely politically expedient, but rather are upright and godly.

3. We pray for all the churches in our city, O God; cause them to seek you with all their hearts on behalf of our city, asking that you would turn the hearts of the inhabitants to you.
4. As the preaching of Jonah caused the rulers of Nineveh to repent and turn to God, bring godly fear on our rulers, and cause them to turn to you, O God, we pray.
5. Save our city, O Lord, and cause a widespread revival to begin and spread out around this nation and to other nations of the world.

9th Isaiah 54:13-14
Children's spiritual life

1. We pray for all our parents, O God, that each would have the wisdom to bring up their children in the ways of the Lord.
2. Help our parents to be godly examples to their children, so that they may see the example of their parents, and choose to follow Christ for themselves.
3. Give our parents wisdom to lead family devotions each day, and the wisdom to be able to explain the answers from a biblical point of view to any questions their children raise.
4. We pray that our children will grow to become men and women who are mighty in the Spirit of God, and in handling the Scriptures.
5. Holy Spirit, as we seek to show them the right pathways, we ask you to directly teach our children, and impress upon them the ways of God and the truth of his Word, so that they may know your voice when you speak to them.

10th Isaiah 54:15-17
God's protection

1. Lord, help us to walk so closely to you in all we do, that we never give the devil a foothold or a fingerhold into any part of our lives.

2. If there are any grey areas in our individual lives, or in the life of the church, that grant access to the powers of darkness   , we repent and confess them before you now, so that we may know the full blessing of God.
3. Search us, Holy Spirit, and help us to put on the full armour of God: the helmet of salvation; breastplate of righteousness; shoes of readiness to spread the Gospel; belt of truth; sword of the Spirit, and the shield of faith.
4. We pray for ourselves and any we know who may be going through a time of trial where the oppression of the enemy is felt; give us strength to overcome, we pray.
5. We take authority over any evil spirits that are currently seeking to come against the church or anyone within it, and rebuke them now in Jesus' Name.

 11th Isaiah 55:1-2
The spiritually thirsty and spiritually hungry

1. Lord, give us an ever deeper thirst for you and for your ways, so that we may fulfil your purposes in our individual lives, and collectively as a church.
2. As we hunger and thirst after righteousness, O Lord, give us a passion to see our society changed, and for us to both pray and act to enable that to happen.
3. May we never stop seeking your face for you to move to bring the revival to our society, O God, for this is also your heart.
4. Give us the joy, O Lord, of being able to bring the unsaved to a knowledge of salvation in Christ, who is the Bread of Life.
5. Thank you, Heavenly Father, that you supply all our needs according to your glorious riches in Christ Jesus.

 Isaiah 55:3-4
Listening to God

1. Lord, help us not to be always so busy that we forget to spend time listening for your voice.
2. Lord, may our busyness, even if it is busyness in your work, never be a substitute for the time needed to wait on you in prayer, which enables you to speak to us.
3. Help us to know your voice, to listen to it, and to obey when you speak to us, O Lord.
4. If you are speaking to us, Lord, and we are not listening, then do what is necessary to gain our attention, even if that is a painful procedure for us.
5. Since obedience is better than sacrifice, help us to put obedience to you at the top of our priorities, so that we may be fruitful and you may be blessed with your children, O Lord.

 Isaiah 55:5
Praying for the nations in our midst

1. We pray for all those from the nations of Europe in our midst; cause them to acknowledge their need of the Saviour, and accept Christ.
2. We pray for all those from African nations in our midst; may those who do not yet know you, O God, find you through the witness of your Church.
3. We pray for all those from the countries in the continent of Asia, in our midst, that each one will be witnessed to, and that the Holy Spirit would open their hearts to receive the Gospel and be saved.
4. We pray for all those in our midst from the north and south continents of America, and the West Indian islands, O Lord; touch their hearts and save them, we ask.

5. We pray for all those in our midst from Australasia, and all the individual island nations, that you would bring them to a knowledge of yourself, O Lord.

 Isaiah 55:6
Seeking the Lord

1. Teach us to seek a deep and intimate relationship with you, O God.
2. May we get to know more of the fatherhood of God towards us, and how it can affect us and change us.
3. Lord Jesus, may we know you more and more as our Good Shepherd, and become more intimately acquainted with your voice.
4. Holy Spirit, teach us more of the ways of God, and help us surrender more and more to you, so that you can transform us more into the image and character of Christ.
5. As we seek first the Kingdom of God and your righteousness, may all that we need be added to us, we pray.

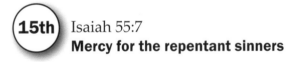 Isaiah 55:7
Mercy for the repentant sinners

1. For any ungodly thoughts that we may be harbouring, O Lord, forgive us and help us to change.
2. For all the friends we meet with regularly, who have not yet given their lives to Christ, save them, O Lord, we pray.
3. We pray for our lawmakers, O God, that they would recognise that the headlong rush to pass ungodly laws only brings harm to the nation and to individuals.
4. We pray for all the churches up and down the land, that the true undiluted Gospel may be preached in boldness and in power, resulting in the salvation of the ungodly.

5. We pray for all those we know or live amongst, who have a lifestyle of crime; cause them to change their ways and come to the place of repentance, O God.

 16th Isaiah 55:8-9
Discerning God's thoughts and ways

1. Reveal to us your thoughts, O God, and teach us to think as you do.
2. Lord, your Word says we can know the mind of Christ; help us to think not carnal thoughts that are based on human reason, but spiritual thoughts that are based on faith.
3. Reveal your ways to us, Holy Spirit, that we may live lives that more and more reflect the character and actions of Christ.
4. Give us a faith that is childlike and so trusts your Word, so that we can step out in faith and without fear, as you lead us in your ways.
5. Forgive us, O Lord, when our minds and human reasoning get in the way of the great things you want to do in and through us; may we instead, like Peter, be able to 'step out of the boat'.

 17th Isaiah 55:10-11
The power of God's Word

1. Lord, help us not to neglect your Word, but rather to prioritise our time day by day, so we can devote a portion of each day to reading your Word.
2. Let us not be merely hearers of your Word, O Lord, but also doers of it; let your Word change us daily as we obey it, and allow it to transform our minds, characters and actions.
3. Give us the faith to be able to stand boldly upon the promises in your Word without doubting, and so see you work miracles through each of us.

4. Lord, as we pray through the Scriptures, which are the Word of God, we pray that we will not only see powerful answers to prayer, but also that our faith level and expectation will rise, so that we grow more confident in exercising our faith.
5. We pray for every prophetic word spoken over our individual lives, and over the life of the church; let them come to be, we pray, O God, and let us see you glorified as a consequence, in our individual lives and in the church.

18th Isaiah 55:12-13
The joy of the Lord

1. Lord, let our hearts be continually filled with joy, which is not based merely on outward circumstances, but rather is the fruit of the Spirit, and which comes from our relationship with you.
2. Cause us not to quench your Spirit, but rather to allow him to have full sway within us, so that our joy may be full.
3. Since obedience is better than sacrifice, and joy comes from walking in obedience to you, O Lord, help us not to stray from your ways, so that our joy may be full.
4. Give us the joy of winning people to Christ, and seeing them surrender their lives in obedience to him, we pray.
5. When we feel weak, may the joy of the Lord be our strength.

19th Isaiah 56:1
Justice

1. Help us, O Lord, to act justly, to love mercy, and to walk humbly before our God, so that we may be pleasing in your sight, O Lord.
2. Cause us to see the best in others, rather than just condemning them, O God.
3. We have received great mercy from you, O God; enable us, in turn, to treat others with mercy, even if they do not deserve it, so that we can walk in the ways of Christ.

4. As we have received the righteousness that comes through accepting Christ as our Saviour and Lord, give us a passion to bring that same experience to those who are currently living lives of sin, O Lord.
5. Rise up in our midst, Lord Jesus, and let your righteousness be revealed in and through us, and in the midst of your Church, we cry.

 Isaiah 56:2
Honouring God

1. Lord, may you always be our first priority.
2. Holy Spirit, convict us if we should find ourselves neglecting the assembling of ourselves together to meet you in collective worship, in accordance with your Word.
3. As we come to worship together each Sunday, enable us to prepare our hearts, so that we come ready to give and not merely to receive.
4. Lord, may no idol come in our way that would distract us from the need to meet collectively for worship each week.
5. As we meet each week in collective worship, O Lord, may your presence be so real amongst us, that we witness sinners getting saved; the sick being healed, and all kinds of situations being turned around for good, because you are in our midst.

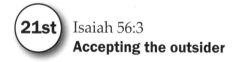 Isaiah 56:3
Accepting the outsider

1. Lord, we thank you that you are calling men and women out from every nation into the one family of God, through our faith in Jesus Christ.
2. We pray for all the immigrants in our nation, who have come here already saved and knowing Christ; may they influence this nation for good by their prayers, their evangelism, and their witness for Jesus.

3. We pray for all the immigrants in this nation we know, and who have come here without knowing Christ; may you cause them to hear the Gospel and be saved, O Lord.
4. We pray for all students who have come here for a short time just to study, but who come from countries where they have never heard the Gospel of Christ's love and salvation; save them before they return to their own nations, O God.
5. Give us the wisdom, O Lord, to be able to share the Good News of Jesus with those of other cultures who live around us, in a way that is relevant, meaningful and effective.

 Isaiah 56:4-7
Blessings for the unfortunate

1. We pray for all those in the church, who do not feel they are able to do much for God; cause them to understand their position in Christ, and the authority that has been delegated to them to use in this lifetime, we pray.
2. Cause us to keep our eyes always fixed on the future; to understand the glorious future of eternity in the presence of the Lord and, as a consequence, to see any present trials as merely light and momentary afflictions.
3. May we always remember that you, O Lord, count being faithful to our calling as disciples of Christ as being far more important than what the world would count 'success'; keep us faithful, we pray.
4. For all of us, may worship be a lifestyle and not merely something that happens on a Sunday.
5. Strengthen the bonds of unity between us, O Lord, that at all times there may be unity amidst our diversity as the family of God.

 Isaiah 56:8
Praying for Israel

1. We pray for the peace of Jerusalem, O Lord, and look forward to the day you will cause all swords to be turned into ploughshares, and all spears to be turned into pruning hooks.
2. We pray for all the Israelis living in Israel, who have little belief in God at all; have mercy on these children of Abraham, and reveal your presence and saving power to them, O God.
3. We pray for all the inhabitants of Israel, who acknowledge God but who have rejected Christ as their Saviour; open their eyes to the truth of Christ, even as Jesus is so clearly prophesied in the book of Isaiah.
4. We pray for all Jews in all parts of the world; cause them to find Jesus as their one true Messiah.
5. We pray for all those who are not Jews, but who live in Israel; thank you for those you have already saved, and we pray that more and more will respond to the Gospel and accept Christ as Saviour.

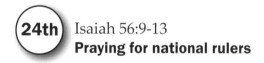 Isaiah 56:9-13
Praying for national rulers

1. We pray for our Prime Minister and our national Government; help them to govern not as men-pleasers, but rather convict their consciences, so that they govern with righteousness.
2. We pray for each Member of Parliament, that they would seek to uphold that which is just, fair and godly in our land.
3. We pray for the Mayor of our city to have an encounter with the risen Christ; to be thoroughly changed, and to lead in the ways of righteousness, O Lord.
4. We pray for all our local councillors; may the local church start to have a greater and greater influence over their policies, so that they pursue ways that are right and pleasing to God.
5. Send revival in our midst, O God, and to our nation, we pray.

Isaiah 57:1
Praying for those oppressed for following Jesus

1. We pray for the rulers of those nations that actively reject Christ and persecute those who follow Jesus; Lord, in your mercy, visit those nations with your saving power, we pray.
2. We pray for all those nations that forbid the opening of any churches or Christians meeting together; open up the doors, we pray, for the Gospel to penetrate those nations in power.
3. We pray for all Christians, who are being persecuted and killed simply because they believe in Jesus; give them grace and strength in their times of trial, we pray.
4. We pray for all the families of those who are bereaved because their loved ones have been killed for following Jesus; help them in their distress, we pray.
5. We pray for all those in our own country, who are persecuted in different ways because they want to follow Christ and live according to his standards, and not according to the ways of this world.

 Isaiah 57:2
Walking uprightly

1. Help us to walk uprightly, O Lord, seeking to please you and not to please men.
2. Cause us to grow daily in the grace of Christ, so that we are being transformed into his likeness with ever-increasing glory.
3. May the God who said, "Let light shine out of darkness" make his light to so shine in our hearts that the light of the knowledge of Christ shines through.
4. Help us, O Lord, at all times in all our dealings, whether at work, with people or in church, always to act with total integrity of heart and mind.

5. Thank you, O God, that you are our Shield who bestows favour, and that you withhold no good thing from those who walk uprightly; help us to walk in that divine favour daily.

 Isaiah 57:3-4
Praying for those caught up in the occult

1. We pray for all those we know who are caught up in the occult in its various forms; have mercy on them, and cause them to turn to the true Source of spiritual power.
2. We pray for all those who need deliverance; open their eyes to their need, and cause them to find total release and freedom in Christ.
3. We pray for our Deliverance Team; help and strengthen them at all times, we pray, as they regularly help people to be set free from demonic strongholds.
4. For any demonic strongholds that seek to influence, hold back, or hinder the work of your church, we take authority over them right now in Jesus' Name, and break their influence and power right now.
5. We take authority right now over any who are using witchcraft against the church or any individuals within the church, and bind their power and influence totally in Jesus' Name.

 Isaiah 57:5a
Praying for those with a lifestyle of sexual immorality

1. We pray for any in the church who are caught up in any kind of sexually immoral practices; convict them, and bring them into the joy of obedience to your Word, O Lord.
2. For any who are caught up in or are tempted by adultery, cause them to repent and turn back to you, O God.
3. For all those who know you, O Lord, but who still do not live lives that are clean before you; Holy Spirit, help them to surrender wholly to God.

4. We pray that the Holy Spirit will be so powerfully present amongst us that all those living a lifestyle of immorality will be convicted and change.
5. Help us to live according to the ways of God, which lead to peace and joy, and not according to the ways of this world, which lead only to destruction.

 29th Isaiah 57:5b
Praying for those who sacrifice children

1. We pray for our nation that actively permits and encourages abortion; have mercy on us, O Lord, for our sinful ways.
2. We pray for all our children and youth in this nation, who are taught sexual permissiveness without reference to morality or the harm that can ensue; have mercy on this nation, O Lord, and bring us back to our senses.
3. We pray for all the doctors and nurses, who daily carry out abortions; have mercy on them, and cause them to understand the reality of what they are doing.
4. Have mercy on this generation of adults that has taught its children sexual immorality and, in so doing, has been responsible for ruining many a young life.
5. Have mercy on this nation, whose children and youth are growing up without boundaries, love or discipline; we need you to move in revival, O God.

 30th Isaiah 57:6
Praying for those who mock God

1. Have mercy on those in our media who mock God; have mercy on them, and save them before they have to stand before you in judgment.
2. We pray for all those we know who profess to be atheists and so spurn their Creator; give us the wisdom we need as we speak to them, and may they be saved, we pray.

3. Rise up in our midst, O God, and may your power be demonstrated through the lives of your people, so the world can see that you are real.

4. Give us the faith to be able to take you at your Word, and to move in the signs and wonders that confound the mockers.

5. O God, save our city, our nation and all the people of this land, we pray; turn the mockery of mockers into worship, by bringing them to the saving knowledge of Jesus Christ.

66 Your ear hears our cry for
the revival of your Church in
this nation, and we pray once again
for you to have mercy and cause
your Church to rise up in power
across this land, O God. **99**

(July 16)

July

Praying for the Church to Arise to the Challenge of the Hour

Isaiah Chapters 58 to 60

Isaiah had received his vision of the Lord on his throne, and had offered himself for service, as recorded in Isaiah Chapter 6. God commissions him as a prophet to the nation of Israel and to other nations. But the God who knows the future told Isaiah right at the beginning how Isaiah's ministry would be received by the people he was being sent to preach to. They would "be ever hearing, but never understanding; be ever seeing, but never perceiving" (Isaiah 6:9). In other words, nobody was going to listen to what Isaiah would say to them, even though he was speaking the undoubted Word of God.

His preaching over the next forty years of his ministry would include some incredibly accurate prophecies about the fate of great nations; personal prophecies into the lives of individuals; detailed prophecies of the coming of the Messiah, his ministry and substitutionary death and resurrection, and right down to the time of the final destruction of the earth as we now know it. He is regarded

> **The people would "be ever hearing, but never understanding; be ever seeing, but never perceiving"**

We still have time, if the Church responds in intercessory prayer for repentance in this nation

as the loftiest of the Old Testament-writing prophets, whose prophecies, like his initial calling, took him into the heavenly places.

And yet, for all that, nobody listened to or responded to his preaching, even though he preached during a ministry of over forty years. Hebrews 11:37 makes reference to how Isaiah's life ended. He was put into a hollow tree trunk and sawn in two. He was one of those many prophets who were "persecuted and mistreated – the world was not worthy of them" (Hebrews 11:37-38). Although his words fell largely on deaf ears, this did not stop him preaching God's Word. That vision early in his life of the God of holiness on his throne, and Isaiah's own sense of personal sinfulness in God's presence, drove him continually to warn a people to turn from their sin.

His prophecies, of course, came true: the prosperity of the people crumbled, and the nation fell into ruin.

Our nation is in a dire situation, spiritually. It needs to forsake its immoral and ungodly ways, and turn back to the Lord before it becomes too late. We still have time, if the Church responds in intercessory prayer for repentance in this nation.

As we continue to pray through Isaiah, we are praying for the Church to rise up to the challenge of the hour and for national revival.

• • • • • • • • • • • • • • • • • •

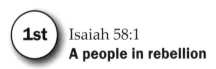 Isaiah 58:1
A people in rebellion

1. Lord, forgive your Church for all the times your Word and your ways have not been followed; revive us, your Church, we pray.

2. Lord, forgive us when we have failed to stand up for the truth, but have allowed wickedness to take root, by our standing idly by and doing nothing; cause your Church to rise up before it is too late.

3. Lord, forgive your Church for being willing to compromise with the ways of the world, instead of making a stand for the truth, and raise up spiritual leaders throughout our nation to turn the Church back to the ways of God.

4. Lord, cause a great vacuum to grow in the lives of the population of this nation that will result in them realising it can only be filled by a relationship with a supernatural God, and turn them to Christ as Saviour and Lord.

5. Lord, as there continues to be an increase in the rate of violence, crime, immorality, disrespect for all forms of authority, and a lack of discipline, let our lawmakers realise the folly of turning away from biblical, moral principles, and cause our nation to start to cry out for change for the better.

 2nd Isaiah 58:2
A form of religion without the power of God

1. Lord, deliver us from being content to focus on the outward trappings of religion only, which thereby lacks any power or influence with you.

2. When we seek you in prayer, O Lord, may our efforts not be fruitless, because we are asking with the wrong motives; rather, give us the mind of Christ, so that we can ask in prayer those things you want to hear and answer.

3. Lord, keep us from being hearers of your Word only, but not doers of it; may we put your Word and will into action.

4. When we are able to act contrary to your Word and will, without conviction of wrongdoing because our hearts have become hardened, Holy Spirit, convict us of sin so we can come back in line with your will.

5. May our desire to seek you come not from the motive of selfish gain, but from unselfish and unconditional love for you, O God.

3rd Isaiah 58:3
Fasting

1. Lord, move us with pity for the unsaved and for the lost of our nation, that we seek you with all our heart in prayer, intercession, supplication and fasting.
2. Lead us by your Spirit, and give us wisdom when to fast, when not to, and for how long, that we may always do it for the right reasons.
3. Cause us, O Lord, to be right before you on the inside, so that our attitudes are pleasing to you, and so when we fast and pray, we can do so effectively and powerfully.
4. Lord, your Word says that those who may dwell in your sanctuary are those who speak the truth from the heart; who do not slander, and who do their neighbour no wrong; guide us daily, Holy Spirit, in the ways of God.
5. Lord, your Word says that those who may dwell in your sanctuary are those who honour and fear the Lord, and who keep their word even when it hurts; give us strength to be the people you expect us to be.

4th Isaiah 58:4
Unity

1. How good and how pleasant it is when the people of God dwell in unity; remove from within us any cause or potential cause of disunity, so that your Holy Spirit may move freely amongst us in power, O Lord.
2. We pray for any family in the church, where there may be strife between husband and wife; Holy Spirit, convict them of sin and bring submission to the Lordship of Christ, and thereby bring restoration of family unity.
3. We pray for all the husbands in our church, that they may always be considerate to their wives and treat them with respect, so that nothing will hinder their prayers.

4. We pray for all the wives in the church, that they may always treat their husbands with respect, so that their witness will not fall into disrepute.
5. We pray for any family in the church, where there may be strife between parent and child; cause both parties to walk in your ways, and bring peace where there is division, we pray.

5th Isaiah 58:5
Walking in humility

1. Lord Jesus, you showed us the pattern for those who desire to follow you when you left Heaven's glory; humbled yourself, and came not to be served but to serve; teach us to walk in your ways.
2. When we act out of pride, Holy Spirit, convict us, and give us the humility to recognise it and to change.
3. Teach us the power of humbling ourselves before you, O Lord, and your power that you can allow to flow through us as a consequence, O God.
4. Teach us the difference between meekness and weakness, O Lord, so that we may not be weak and ineffective, but rather humble and powerful.
5. Help us to understand and accept the circumstances you allow to come into our lives that may hurt our pride, but which are designed to help us to grow spiritually and in power.

6th Isaiah 58:6
Acting justly

1. We pray for all those in the church, who are employers; may they always treat their employees justly and in a manner pleasing to you, O Lord.
2. We pray for all those in the church, who have positions of authority over others in their places of work; cause each one to honour you, O Lord, by acting justly and fairly at all times.

3. We pray for all the parents in the church; help them never to exasperate their children by inconsistent or unfair treatment, but rather to bring them up consistently in the training and instruction of the Lord.
4. Give us the grace to be able to drop claims we may have against people, even if justified, when it would be a better witness than seeking our own gain.
5. Give us an empathetic heart that is always able to stand in the shoes of the other person, and so feel as they do; and thereby give us the grace to act with justice and mercy in every situation.

7th Isaiah 58:7
Generous givers

1. Break any spirit of poverty that any of us may be afflicted by, O Lord, so that we can give freely and generously, without fear of suffering loss.
2. Teach us to trust fully in you and in your Word, by giving to you our tithes and offerings with a glad heart.
3. Cause us always to have listening ears to those less fortunate than ourselves, so that we do not close our ears to them in their time of need.
4. Cause us to remember what you said, Lord Jesus, that it is "more blessed to give than to receive".
5. Forgive us, O Lord, if we are rich in possessions, but poor spiritually because of our unchristlike attitudes and behaviour; bring change to our attitudes and spiritual poverty, we pray.

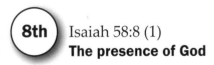

8th Isaiah 58:8 (1)
The presence of God

1. O Holy Spirit, teach us as the people of God to walk so closely to you that the presence of Jesus will be seen clearly in each of us, and your power will work through us.

2. O Lord, cause us to continue to seek you in prayer and to conform to your ways, so that the presence of God will become more and more obvious and noticeable in our meetings.

3. We pray that the presence of God will be such that the unsaved will be convicted of sin and turn to Christ; the backsliders will be turned around, and each of us will be moved to get closer to you in all that we do.

4. Holy Spirit, we ask that your presence will be so close to us that we may be clearly guided by you in all our decision-making, in our lives and in our evangelism; speak to us, regularly giving us ears to hear what the Spirit is saying.

5. O Holy Spirit, we ask that as we witness to others, whether at home, at work or on the streets, that your presence will be so strong upon us that you will bring such conviction to those we talk to that they will be saved.

9th Isaiah 58:8 (2)
God's healing

1. Thank you, Lord, for every testimony of healing we hear; we pray that you would move more and more powerfully amongst us to heal the sick.

2. We pray that we will see more and more healings on the streets, as we take the Gospel out to the unsaved.

3. Give us the courage and the boldness to pray for the sick with an expectant faith, we pray, O Lord, and to see it as a means of reaching the lost.

4. We pray for all our Discipleship Cells that the power of God would be very real and evident, as the sick are prayed for and recover in the Name of Jesus.

5. We pray for all those we know, who have been suffering sickness for a long time; we pray that you would touch them right now and heal them, O Lord.

10th Isaiah 58:8 (3)
The glory of God

1. Lord, may our lives be so lived out in accordance to your will, that you are glorified in our lives both as individuals and as a congregation.
2. When we meet for collective worship, may we come with hearts prepared, so that Jesus may have the pre-eminence, and all men and women will be drawn to him.
3. Cause us to remember, O God, that we are created first and foremost for the glory of God; by your Spirit, enable us to live up to that high calling, we ask.
4. Let the glory of God be evident at all our Discipleship Cell meetings, so that others will see and desire to know this awesome God whom we serve.
5. As we witness to those of other religions, who are trying to find and please God by their own works, we pray that they may see the glory of Christ within us, and desire to have what we have.

11th Isaiah 58:9
Being heard by God

1. Lord, you know our every word even before we have spoken them, and you know our every prayer; may we, in every situation, pray as Jesus would have prayed, and so be heard by God.
2. Thank you, Lord, for every answer to prayer that we can testify to; hear us today as we bring all our needs before you, and when you answer, may we testify to your faithfulness.
3. When we cry to you for our nation to turn back once more to you, O Lord, hear our prayer, and save our nation from self-destruction.
4. When we cry to you to save those we are praying for, who have not yet surrendered their lives to you, O God, hear and answer our prayer, we ask.

5. We bring all our personal prayer requests to you right now, O Lord, and ask that you minister to each one by your grace and in your power.

 Isaiah 58:10
Concern for others

1. Lord, in accordance with your will, help us to love our neighbours as ourselves, giving us a heart of concern and compassion.
2. Lord Jesus, you taught us that it is right to go the extra mile; help us to have the eyes to see the needs of others, and the grace to be like you in meeting those needs.
3. In every area of our daily lives, help us to be conscious of those you would have us help, either by an encouraging word or by some practical action, and may Jesus be seen in us by those to whom we minister.
4. Lord, help us to remember that each person we meet, no matter who they are, is created in your image, and you desire to save them; help us to see all people as you see them.
5. Whenever we are asked for help, or for money, may our first thought not be to refuse, but rather to seek to help.

 Isaiah 58:11
Our needs met

1. Thank you, Lord, that when we obey your Word we do not become impoverished but always enriched.
2. Give us this day our daily bread, and all other things that are necessary for daily life, we pray.
3. Guide us continually in all the small decisions of our daily lives, and also with all the big decisions; and we bring before you right now our major decisions and ask for your direction.
4. Teach us to be generous with our worldly goods, so that you can be generous in meeting all our worldly needs.

5. Cause us, O God, to remember your Word that teaches us that we reap in accordance with what we sow; may we be generous sowers, so that you can raise up a rich harvest.

 Isaiah 58:12
Restoration

1. We pray for all those in the church we know, who need to be healed emotionally; touch them, and minister to their deepest needs right now, we pray.
2. We pray for the non-Christians we know, who need emotional healing and a radical change in their domestic circumstances; help them, we ask, and help us to be part of the answer to their need.
3. Cause us not to be peace*keepers*, but rather peace*makers*, so that we actively seek to bring about reconciliation to fractured relationships.
4. We pray for any believers we know, who are out of fellowship with each other for whatever reason; cause them to be reconciled and their relationship restored.
5. We pray for all non-Christian family and friends we know, who are experiencing broken relationships; we pray they will experience full restoration, and that they also find peace with God through Jesus Christ.

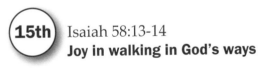 Isaiah 58:13-14
Joy in walking in God's ways

1. O God, let the joy of the Lord be our strength continually, whether we are in good circumstances or not so good.
2. May we not allow the busyness or the problems of life to so overtake us that we neglect the regular meeting together to worship and praise our God.

3. We pray for the times of worship in the church; may your anointing be ever increasing and transporting us into times of great joy, as we worship our living Saviour.
4. We pray for a great anointing upon the times of worship in our Discipleship Cells, as the presence of God grows stronger.
5. As we seek you in our personal times of devotion, O Lord, may we continue to grow ever closer to you and, in the process, experience more of the joy that comes from our relationship with you.

 Isaiah 59:1
The God of the impossible

1. O God, you can do all things; cause our faith to rise up to understand that you are the God of the impossible.
2. We bring before you now every situation that needs prayer for what, to men, seems impossible; help and undertake for each situation we now bring before you, we ask.
3. Your ear hears our cry for the revival of your Church in this nation, and we pray once again for you to have mercy and cause your Church to rise up in power across this land, O God.
4. Your ear hears our cry to turn our nation around and back to God, and once again we pray for your grace to touch this nation, and cause all those who do not yet know you to find Jesus as Lord and Saviour.
5. Lord, your arm is able to reach out and save the lost; we bring before you now every person we know, who is drowning in their sins and needs the arm of the Lord to reach out and rescue them.

 Isaiah 59:2-3
Forgiveness needed

1. Lord, we bring every iniquity that we have committed before you now, and ask for your forgiveness.

2. Lord, we bring all the iniquities of our nation before you now, and ask for your forgiveness.
3. Lord, we bring all the iniquities of our forefathers before you now, and ask for your forgiveness.
4. Lord, we bring all the sins of your Church before you, and ask for your forgiveness and for hearts of total repentance.
5. If there is any barrier between us and you, O Lord, caused by any unforgiveness in our hearts, we confess it now, and release those people right now from our resentment.

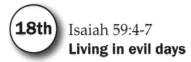 Isaiah 59:4-7
Living in evil days

1. Lord, we pray for our justice system; for the lawmakers; for the police, and for the magistrates and judges in our Courts; may they do their duty, acting with wisdom and justice, we pray.
2. Holy Spirit, move in our neighbourhood and in our streets, we pray, bringing the presence of Jesus there that banishes the powers of darkness.
3. We pray for all those in our neighbourhood who engage in crime; cause them to hear the Gospel and be saved and totally transformed, we pray.
4. We pray for all those in our neighbourhood who are addicted to drugs; have mercy on them, and help them to find a totally new life in Christ.
5. We pray for all the drug dealers in our neighbourhood; save those who are willing to respond to the Gospel, and drive out those who are not.

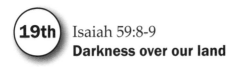 Isaiah 59:8-9
Darkness over our land

1. Rise up, O Prince of Peace, Light of the world, Lord Jesus Christ, and shine in this place, banishing the darkness of evil.

2. Cause us, your people, to shine brightly for Christ in the spiritual darkness that surrounds us, O God.
3. We pray that the light of the Gospel of Jesus Christ would break out in every part of our nation once again.
4. Turn back the tide of evil that has been swamping our land, O Lord, and scatter your enemies that would keep this nation in captivity to sin and darkness.
5. Turn back the tide of humanism, false religions, the occult and New Age practices that conspire together to keep the nation from finding the light of Christ and the eternal life that the Gospel brings.

 Isaiah 59:10-11
The blind leading the blind

1. The eyes of our national leaders are blind, O Lord, as they seek to please men and not God; let there be a shaking in our nation that will cause their eyes to be opened to the truth of God.
2. The forces of 'political correctness' seek to stifle the proclamation of the Gospel in this land; break the spiritual strongholds that lie behind it, we pray.
3. We pray for every town hall and local authority up and down our country; open their eyes to the folly of acting contrary to the revealed laws of God, we pray.
4. We pray for all church leaders who do not have a personal relationship with God, but rather act only out of a sense of religious practice; save them, and turn their lives around, we pray.
5. We pray for all church leaders who do not preach the Gospel, and who do not believe the Bible to be the Word of God; have mercy on them, and let them have a 'Damascus road' experience with the risen Christ, O Lord.

21st Isaiah 59:12-13
Seeking mercy for sin

1. Lord, we repent for all the times we have failed to make a stand for Christ; forgive us, we pray.
2. Lord, we repent on behalf of the Church that has failed to make a stand for the truth over recent generations; forgive us, we pray.
3. Lord, we repent on behalf of our governments over the past decades that have turned away from your righteous ways; forgive and have mercy, we pray.
4. Lord, we repent on behalf of our forefathers, who began to turn away from God and have allowed a generation to grow up largely ignorant of the truth of the Bible and of Christ; forgive and have mercy, we pray.
5. Lord, have mercy on this nation; remember how it once followed your ways, and restore this nation back to you, we pray.

22nd Isaiah 59:14-15
Preaching the truth

1. Lord, make every person in the church a bold and powerful witness of the life-changing power of Jesus Christ, and give each one opportunities to share the Gospel with others.
2. We pray for the preaching of your Word from the pulpit each Sunday, that it would always come forth in power, and with signs and wonders of salvation of souls; healing of the sick, and lives and situations radically changed as a consequence.
3. We pray for our Discipleship Cells, that the power and the preaching of God's Word would manifest itself in salvation, healings and radical life-changing situations taking place as a regular occurrence.
4. Make us a church that is not confined to a building, but rather, wherever your people are, the power of God may be present to save, heal and change lives.

5. Open up opportunities for your people to be placed in positions of great influence in their places of work, and in all other areas of society, and to have the boldness to be witnesses and to spread the Gospel in a way that changes our society.

 Isaiah 59:16-17
Putting on spiritual armour

1. Lord, help us to ensure that we do not neglect the spiritual armour you have made available to us, so that the enemy may never gain a foothold.
2. Lord, help us not to neglect the breastplate of righteousness, but to walk only according to your standards of righteousness.
3. Help us to ensure our minds are always guarded by the helmet of salvation, so that we are not tempted to backslide.
4. As we put on the belt of truth, help us to be people who are totally trustworthy, just as Jesus has always been totally trustworthy.
5. Let our feet be continually shod ready to go and spread the Gospel, and may we never drop the guard of our shield of faith in all that we do.

 Isaiah 59:18-19
The wrath of God

1. Lord, may our knowledge that there is a Day of Judgment, which cannot be escaped, cause us to have a compassion for the lost, and a desire to see them rescued before it is too late.
2. Lord, may our knowledge that you are a righteous God who hates sin - and therefore, as a righteous Judge, must punish sin - cause us not to live carelessly as followers of Jesus.
3. Thank you, Lord, that you have done all that is necessary for men and women to escape punishment for sin, and to be saved through the work of Christ on the cross; give listening ears to those with whom we share the Gospel, so that they may be saved.

4. We pray for all those who seek the destruction of the Jews and the nation of Israel, a nation you have called out and whose land you have given to them; have mercy on the unbelieving Jews and on their enemies also, and cause them to be saved, we pray.
5. We pray for all those who kill Christians in the belief they are doing you, Lord, a service; like Saul of Tarsus, show them the truth of the risen Saviour, we pray.

25th Isaiah 59:20
The Redeemer in Zion

1. We pray for all the Messianic Jews, that you would encourage and strengthen them, and help them to reach their fellow Jews with the Gospel of their Saviour, Jesus Christ.
2. We pray for the peace of Jerusalem, O Lord, as your Word encourages us to do; have mercy on that troubled region of the Middle East.
3. We pray for all those who are seeking to spread the Gospel in Israel; grant them safety and success, and fruit from their labours, we pray.
4. We pray for all the Gospel TV and radio programmes in Arabic that are reaching all the Arab nations that surround Israel; anoint those programmes, and cause many of the viewers and listeners to receive Jesus Christ as Saviour.
5. We pray for all the Christians in the Middle Eastern countries, who are being persecuted for following Christ; help, strengthen and encourage them, we pray.

26th Isaiah 59:21
Walking in the Spirit

1. Lord, we thank you for the Holy Spirit, and we ask right now for a fresh infilling each day, so that the anointing within us may flow out to others around us daily.

2. Guide and lead us each day, Holy Spirit, everywhere we go, in all that we do, and in all that we say.

3. For those of us who are not yet baptised in the Holy Spirit, we ask you right now as we pray to give us that good gift that you have promised to those who ask persistently.

4. Let there be a great releasing of the gifts of the Holy Spirit in our midst, O Lord, so that your Church can walk in the demonstration of the power of God, and cause many to be saved as a consequence.

5. Give us the confidence to use those spiritual gifts that you have given us, O Lord, in a way that brings you glory.

 Isaiah 60:1-2
Showing forth God's glory

1. Rise up, O Lord, and let your enemies be scattered in this nation.

2. Rise up, O Lord, and let your enemies be scattered who are at work in our schools, colleges and universities, and who seek to stifle any expression of Christian beliefs and practices.

3. Rise up, O Lord, and let your enemies against the Church be scattered.

4. Rise up, O Lord, and let your enemies against all our missionaries be scattered.

5. Rise up, O Lord, and let your light break all apathy, lukewarmness and lethargy in the Church, so that your Church may demonstrate the glory of a living God.

 Isaiah 60:3-7
God's blessing on the nations

1. Move in mighty power in all the countries of Europe, O Lord, and cause there to be a returning to our Christian roots.

2. Continue to move in revival power across every country of Africa, we pray, from Cape Town to Cairo, and bless and equip all the pastors and church leaders who look after the converts.
3. May the revivals that are taking place in China and South Korea spread out like a mighty fire to engulf every country in the continent of Asia, we pray.
4. May the revivals that are taking place in different parts of South America spread out, and cause the whole continent of North and South America to see revival, O Lord.
5. For Australia and all the island nations, cause a great revival to spread from one land to another, by the power of your Holy Spirit, we pray.

 29th Isaiah 60:8-12

Praying for God's blessing on the nation

1. Lord, have mercy on England, and raise up men and women throughout the country, who will be mighty influencers for Christ in all places of our society.
2. We take authority over all the powers of darkness that are at work in our nation to bring about the breakdown of families; we rebuke you in Jesus' Name, and we pray for the restoration of families.
3. We take authority over every wicked spirit that is at work to bring about lawlessness, crime and a breakdown of all respect for those in positions of authority, whether political leaders, law enforcement, teachers or church leaders; we rebuke you in Jesus' Name, and pray that crime will reduce.
4. We pray that you will raise up influential people in our nation, who will be in such positions of influence in society that they will turn the attitudes of the people of this nation away from unbiblical ways back to the ways of God.
5. Do a miracle in our nation, O God, by removing the veil of blindness that covers the spiritual eyes and ears of the people, and cause them to see and hear the reality of our God.

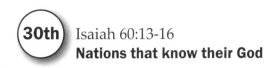 Isaiah 60:13-16
Nations that know their God

1. Lord, we pray for all those nations where we have missionaries working, and pray that you would bless the fruit of their labours.
2. Have mercy on all the Muslim world; let there be a spectacular breakthrough with the Gospel, we pray, and cause countless numbers to come to know the peace that comes through faith in Jesus Christ as Saviour and Lord.
3. Have mercy on all the Hindu world, we pray, and show them how to break free from bondage by turning to the Giver of Life and the Saviour of their souls.
4. We pray for all the Buddhist world, O Lord; send a mighty revival amongst them in these last days that will sweep many into the Kingdom of God.
5. We pray for all those of other religions, spread out in different nations of the world; cause them to hear the Gospel, either by radio, satellite TV, literature or through missionaries, and be saved, and make successful all those who are seeking to reach them with the Gospel.

 Isaiah 60:17-22
Even so, come, Lord Jesus

1. Lord Jesus, let your Kingdom come and let your will be done on earth, as it is in Heaven, we pray.
2. In these last days, despite the evil times that we live in, which the Bible has prophesied would be, nevertheless let the Kingdom of God advance at a spectacular rate, in our midst and before our eyes and in our time, we pray.
3. O Lord, who gives strength to the weary, as we hope in you, may you renew our strength; enable us to soar on wings like eagles; to run and not grow weary; to walk and not be faint.

4. O Lord, for the times we may feel discouraged, enable us to keep our eyes fixed on Jesus, the Author and Perfecter of our faith who, for the joy set before him, endured the cross, scorning its shame, so that we will not grow weary and lose heart.

5. We rejoice, O God, that having disarmed the powers and authorities, Jesus made a public spectacle of them, triumphing over them by the cross; thank you for the total victory there is in Christ.

August

Overcoming Trials of Faith

1 Peter Chapters 1 to 3

When Peter wrote his first letter to the churches, things had begun to change for the worse for the First Century Church. In the early days, the Book of Acts shows Paul and Silas receiving protection from the Roman authorities as they preached the Gospel. But a time of persecution against the Church was about to break out. The Roman Emperor Nero was now in power. Under him, in 64AD, Christians were made a scapegoat, and blamed for the fire that destroyed Rome. This led to many Christians being tortured, crucified and killed in many unpleasant ways, a pattern that was to recur many times in the next 200 years or so. In a short space of time, it would be a crime simply to be a Christian.

Peter wrote his first letter shortly before this first persecution, during which both he and Paul would be executed by Nero: Paul by beheading, and Peter by crucifixion upside down. Peter anticipated the coming persecution. He knew many Christians were puzzled as to why a practising Christian should be subjected to persecution, trials, misunderstandings, dislike and hostility. They were becoming fearful and

In a short space of time, it would be a crime simply to be a Christian

It is also a time of great opportunity for Christians to let their light shine in a dark world

confused, asking questions like, 'Why have misfortunes come into my life?', 'Why does God allow such things for Christians?', 'How do I cope with such problems?'

Peter wrote his first letter to encourage all the churches, stressing that they are God's chosen people, and sufferings are permitted by God purely as a temporary testing and refining of faith. They were not to be disturbed by the malice and misunderstanding shown towards them, but rather to disarm criticism by conduct in every part of life, which reflects the Christian's holy calling. The letter answers two questions the Christians were asking:

1. Why are the problems and trials in my life happening to me?
2. How should I conduct myself as a Christian in the face of such trials?

Our prayer points for this month minister into the situation of Christians, who have to live in a fallen world that is growing steadily more hostile to the preaching and the practice of the truth of the Gospel. And yet it is also a time of great opportunity for Christians to let their light shine in a dark world, and to demonstrate the new life in Christ. "Christ in you - the Hope of glory" (Colossians 1:27).

• • • • • • • • • • • • • • • • • •

1st 1 Peter 1:1-2 (1)
Strangers in the world

1. Lord, cause us at all times to remember that this world is not our home, and that we are only pilgrims passing through to a far better place.

2. Help us to fix our eyes on Jesus, the Author and Perfecter of our faith, so we may run with perseverance the race marked out for us.
3. As we keep our eyes on where we are heading, may it continually strengthen us in all of our momentary trials.
4. Enable us to keep in perspective the temporary nature of this present life and world, compared to the eternal value of what we are yet to experience.
5. Lord, may the knowledge that we are but pilgrims in this world help us to keep a loose hold on worldly things, but a firm grasp on all that is spiritual.

 **2nd** 1 Peter 1:1-2 (2)
God's elect

1. Thank you, Lord, that we love you because you first loved us. May we daily live in a way that reflects our gratitude to you for saving us.
2. Give us grateful hearts of thanksgiving, and forgive us when our hearts have been cold, hard or ungrateful, despite all you have done for us.
3. Cause us to remember with gratitude what you have saved us from, and to be ever willing to tell others of the blessings of salvation through the cross of Christ.
4. For all those believers amongst us, who struggle or doubt the depth of your love for them, we pray they will understand all that it means to be the elect of God.
5. May we so live, that we reflect the truth of your Word that says, "What shall it profit a man if he shall gain the whole world and lose his own soul?"

3rd 1 Peter 1:1-2 (3)
Chosen for obedience

1. Lord, you have saved us to live lives of obedience to you. Forgive our disobedience as we pledge afresh, right now, to walk fully in the ways of God.
2. Holy Spirit, help us to shake off all apathy; to refocus our minds fully on the Lord, and to live lives of obedience to you that therefore bear much fruit and glorify Jesus.
3. Lord, your Word says, "Obedience is better than sacrifice." May we be Spirit-led people and not merely 'religious' people.
4. Not my will, but yours be done in my life, O God.
5. Cause your Church to repent of all times of lack of obedience, and to rise up in the power of the Holy Spirit.

4th 1 Peter 1:3-5 (1)
A living hope

1. Thank you, Lord, that you have revealed what the future holds for the believer. Keep us looking upwards in faith and hope, rather than downwards in doubt and despair.
2. Enable us to focus on our first priority of storing up treasures in Heaven, and only secondly to focus on the treasures on earth, which we also yield to you.
3. When we feel discouraged, Holy Spirit, lift our spirits by bringing to our remembrance all the blessings we already have, and also what we will have in Christ.
4. In times of trials, may we be able to say with Job, "I know that my Redeemer lives...and after my skin has been destroyed, yet in my flesh I will see God."
5. Lord, in times of discouragement, bring to our remembrance your words,"He who believes in me will live, even though he dies; and whoever lives and believes in me will never die."

5th 1 Peter 1:3-5 (2)
Shielded by God's power

1. Thank you, God, that though the powers of darkness may be strong and mighty, by contrast you are omnipotent – the *Al*mighty.
2. Help us never to forget or doubt your all-encompassing power to guard and keep your people and your Church from every attack of the enemy.
3. We bring our minds to you, O Lord, which is the enemy's battleground, and pray we may continually put on the helmet of salvation to guard against every attack.
4. May we take up the shield of faith to extinguish every flaming arrow of the evil one.
5. Keep us praying in the Spirit on all occasions, and with all kinds of prayers and requests, so we may overcome in every situation.

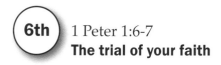

6th 1 Peter 1:6-7
The trial of your faith

1. Lord, help us to be patient in times of trial, remembering that you use these times to mould and strengthen our character.
2. When our faith is tested by trials, may we come out of it at the end like pure and refined gold.
3. We pray for all those we know, who are going through difficult times now; guard and keep their faith, and help them to keep their eyes on you.
4. Keep in the forefront of our minds that "God works all things together for good to those who love him."
5. Forgive us, Lord, when we have complained in the difficult times that have been allowed by you as discipline to help us mature. Give us discerning spirits to see the benefits of trials of our faith.

7th 1 Peter 1:8-9
The salvation of our souls

1. Lord, we thank you for the salvation that comes through the cross of Jesus. May we always be ready to share the Good News of salvation through faith in Christ.
2. Lord, stir up the fire of love for Jesus within our hearts, that we may be passionate about spreading the Gospel to all.
3. Revive your Church, O Lord. Make us like the church in the Book of Acts – reaching out to the lost around us in the power of the Holy Spirit.
4. We pray for every act of personal evangelism by individuals; for teams on the streets; for evangelism in and by the Discipleship Cells; make us effective and fruitful.
5. We pray for all the church's missions overseas – for those we have sent, and for those we support. Encourage them, anoint them, bless them, and make them fruitful.

8th 1 Peter 1:10-12 (1)
The prophetic ministry

1. Thank you, Lord, that you speak by divine revelation to your people. Stir up your gifts within your church.
2. Speak Lord, your servant is listening!
3. Release amongst your church, Holy Spirit, the gift of prophecy to strengthen, encourage and comfort your people.
4. Speak to your people in dreams and visions, O Lord, and give us the wisdom and discernment to rightly divide the word of truth.
5. Bring to our remembrance every prophetic word you have brought to us as individuals and as a church, that we may water them with prayer.

 **9th** 1 Peter 1:10-12 (2)
Strategic spiritual insight

1. Give your church prophetic insight into the spiritual battles in the heavenlies concerning our individual lives, that we may overcome.
2. Give us prophetic insight into the spiritual battles arrayed against us as a church, that we may pull down every stronghold.
3. Give us prophetic insight into the spiritual battles over our area, that we may pray strategically with the authority of the Name of Jesus.
4. Give us prophetic insight into the spiritual battles over our country, that we may pray for a turning back from evil to righteousness.
5. Give us prophetic insight into how to pray effectively for the revival of ourselves, our church, our city and our nation.

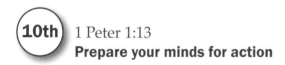 **10th** 1 Peter 1:13
Prepare your minds for action

1. Holy Spirit, help each of us to love the Lord our God with all our heart, soul, strength and mind.
2. Help us to keep our minds fixed on the truly important things in life – spiritual matters – and not to be distracted by secondary and worldly things.
3. Give us discernment that we may always be aware of the plans and devices of our spiritual enemy.
4. Let our minds not become the playground of the enemy, but enable us to banish all thoughts from our minds that are neither of God nor pleasing to God.
5. Let us wait on you, O Lord, that the Holy Spirit may reveal to us the mind of Christ.

11th 1 Peter 1:14
Not conforming to evil desires

1. Lord, forgive the times when we have lapsed into carnality, either in thought, action or speech, and help us to grow in spiritual maturity.
2. We pray for all non-Christians who come to our church, that by your Spirit you would show them the path of righteousness in Christ.
3. We pray for all the carnal Christians in our church, that your Spirit would convict them not to try to live with one foot in the world and one foot in your Kingdom.
4. We pray for all the new Christians in our church, that you would reveal to them those areas they need to change to conform with the ways of Christ.
5. We pray for all the mature Christians in our church, that you would help each one draw nearer to you, and be healthy role models to others in the church.

12th 1 Peter 1:15–16
Be holy, because I am holy

1. Lord, give us your strength to separate ourselves from all the ways of the world that do not conform to the ways of the Kingdom of God.
2. Lord, help us daily to submit our minds, our desires, our plans and our will to you.
3. Lord, we are sinners who have been saved by your grace, and transformed by the power of your Holy Spirit. Enable us to live out a sincere testimony before all people.
4. Holy Spirit, convict us of anything in our lives that is not pleasing to you, and give us the strength to change to conform to your will.

5. Let the fragrance of Jesus flow out from us as we set ourselves apart from sin and unto God.

13th 1 Peter 1:17-19
Live in reverent fear

1. Thank you, Father, that your perfect love casts out all fear of punishment, but help us to have a reverential fear and respect for your holiness and righteousness.
2. Though you will not judge us for our sins, because of our faith in Christ, help us to remember that we will have to give an account of our Christian lives and work. Help us not to be ashamed on that day.
3. Lord, you gave your life and shed your blood for us. We offer our bodies now as living sacrifices as our spiritual act of worship.
4. Heavenly Father, you gave your all for us when you gave Jesus. Forgive us for the times when we have not given you our best, and help us to change today.
5. Teach us to number our days aright that we may gain a heart of wisdom.

14th 1 Peter 1:20-22
Love one another deeply from the heart

1. Lord, first help us to express our love for you with all our being, not just in our words, but in our thoughts and actions.
2. We pray for each of us, who may be struggling with unforgiveness towards those who have hurt or wronged us. Give us the grace to release them fully in forgiveness.
3. For each of us who have taken offence at other people, soften our hearts and teach us to be loving instead of offended.
4. Lord, you said, "A new command I give you: Love one another. As I have loved you, so you must love one another." Teach us to be obedient.

5. Lord, despite all our circumstances, let the love of Christ radiate out from your people, both individually and as a body, and may many come to Christ as a consequence.

15th 1 Peter 1:23-25
Born again

1. Thank you, Lord, for all the blessings of being born again into the Kingdom of God. May we live daily as befits a child of the King of all kings.
2. We pray for all new Christians we know or who are in our care. Help us to encourage them into all spiritual maturity.
3. We pray that week by week, as the Gospel is preached in our Sunday services, that we may continually see people being born again by the Spirit of God.
4. We pray for our Discipleship Cells, that they may see individuals born again and growing in Christ as they reach out to others.
5. We pray for all our individual witnessing to our families, neighbours, students or work colleagues, that we will have the joy of leading others to Christ regularly.

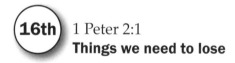

16th 1 Peter 2:1
Things we need to lose

1. Though we are in this world, Lord, give us your grace so that we do not live in accordance with the values of this world.
2. Help us to remember that you are the Judge of all, and that it is not for us to take revenge, but for us to forgive.
3. Keep us from hypocrisy; may our words and our actions always match each other.
4. Enable us to learn the secret of being content in any and every situation, whether we have much or little, so that we are not burdened with envying others.
5. Teach us to put a guard on our mouth, so that only that which is edifying to others, and not slander, passes our lips.

 1 Peter 2:2-3
Crave pure spiritual milk

1. O Lord, may our spirits thirst after you, the Living Water.
2. We pray for those amongst us who struggle to read the Bible. Create in each of us the deep desire to learn more of you from your Word.
3. Give us the self-discipline to take time each day to read and study your Word, so that we may hear from you and learn your ways.
4. Holy Spirit, please reveal more and more spiritual truth each time we read the Bible.
5. Holy Spirit, please lead us into the paths of righteousness, that our lives may reflect Jesus and glorify our Father in Heaven.

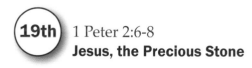 1 Peter 2:4-5
A spiritual house

1. Lord, help us to crucify our old nature, so that our new spiritual nature may take preeminence.
2. Give us the strength to live as led by your Spirit, and not by our fallen nature.
3. Cause us always to remember that we are not our own; we have been bought at a price – the precious blood of Jesus Christ.
4. Come, Lord Jesus, and take your full place in each of our lives as Lord and King.
5. Come, Lord Jesus, and take your place in your Church, and may the world see your glory manifested in all its forms in and through your people.

19th 1 Peter 2:6-8
Jesus, the Precious Stone

1. Jesus, you are the Pearl of Great Price. Teach us to value our relationship with you more and more each day.

2. Forgive us, Lord Jesus, if we have valued anything or anybody more than you. Draw us into your presence.
3. Jesus, just as you and the Father are one, help each of us to become one with our God.
4. O Lord, you who are the Lover of our souls, help us to love you more and more.
5. Teach us the depth of the preciousness of our relationship with our Saviour, and the benefits of his work on the cross.

 1 Peter 2:9-10
Chosen to declare God's praises

1. Help us to remember that we are saved to serve you, and to bring you glory here on earth. May we not fail in our mission.
2. Thank you, Lord, that you have made us a royal priesthood. May we constantly use, and not neglect, the privilege of being able to come boldly before your throne in prayer.
3. Since we have been called to be a holy nation, purge your Church of all that is unholy – and start with us, O Lord.
4. As a people belonging to God, may it be obvious to all, simply by observing our lifestyles and attitudes.
5. Thank you for the mercy you have shown us in saving us, O God. May we, in turn, demonstrate your mercy to others.

 1 Peter 2:11-12
Glorifying God by our deeds

1. Lord, show us all those things in our lives that are not pleasing to you, so that we may remove them.
2. Lord, move in your church revealing all hidden sin, so you may be able to move in power through a holy people.
3. As our evangelistic teams go out to witness and pray for the people on the streets, let the power of your Holy Spirit be mighty upon them, and minister through them to save the lost, heal the sick, and bring hope to the hopeless.

4. We pray for your Holy Spirit to be mightily manifested amongst our Discipleship Cells each time they work together for evangelism, that they will be instrumental in seeing many people saved, restored and growing in Christ.
5. As individual witnesses for Christ, let us so soak in the presence of God, that the presence and power of Jesus can be seen in us by non-believers, so that we can lead them to Christ.

22nd 1 Peter 2:13-17
Obeying the law

1. Remind us, Holy Spirit, that it is God's will that we obey the laws of the land.
2. We pray for those in governmental authority over us; give them wisdom to govern wisely, O Lord.
3. Teach us, in obedience to your will and for the sake of godliness, to show proper respect to all people, whether we think they deserve it or not.
4. Let each of us be model citizens, who are consequently a testimony to all non-believers we work and mix with, who know we can be trusted.
5. May our godly testimony to the world cause people to ask why we are the way we are, so that we can point them to Christ.

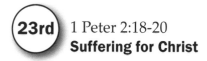

23rd 1 Peter 2:18-20
Suffering for Christ

1. Lord, give us the grace, when it is your will that we go through trying circumstances, to suffer for Christ's sake.
2. Help us understand and discern the times that you allow us to suffer, as helpful discipline that can enable us to grow spiritually if we adopt the right attitude.
3. If we suffer as a result of our own foolish actions, give us the grace to admit it, and to seek your forgiveness and help to change.

4. Help us to be good employees, even when circumstances for us are not good, remembering that whatever we do, we do it as unto God, and may you receive the glory, O Lord.
5. We pray for all believers around the world, who are suffering simply because they are Christians. Help them in their time of need, O God.

 24th 1 Peter 2:21-22
The example of Christ

1. Lord, may we be able to say with the apostle Paul, "Follow my example, as I follow the example of Christ."
2. Teach us to be like Mary, who sat at the feet of Jesus and gained spiritual insight into the plans of God as a consequence.
3. The more we die to self, the more your power can work through us, O Lord. Help us to die to self.
4. Holy Spirit, keep revealing the ways of Christ to each of us more and more, that we may seek to grow more and more like him.
5. Help us, Lord, to truly "go in your Name" to be like Jesus in this world, in character and in the power of the Holy Spirit.

 25th 1 Peter 2:23
Turning the other cheek

1. Help us to control our anger and our words, O Lord, and instead to be a good testimony of your grace that can change our lives.
2. We pray for all those we know, who may be suffering unjustly, whether at work or elsewhere. Give them the strength and grace to trust you to vindicate them.
3. Help us remember your Word that says, "A gentle answer turns away wrath."
4. We pray for all our families, where there is a breakdown of relationships because of unwise words of anger; bring restoration, O Lord, and the humility to change.

5. Instead of reacting with anger, help us to truly trust you, our Father, and allow you to turn our situations around, bringing good out of bad situations.

 1 Peter 2:24-25
Dying to sin

1. Holy Spirit, shine your light into our lives to reveal any sin that we need to put to death.
2. We pray for all those non-Christians who attend our meetings, and who are seeking Christ but have not yet repented. Bring conviction and repentance, O Lord.
3. We pray for those believers in our midst, who are struggling with sin and find it hard to change. Convict them, Holy Spirit, and give them the strength to break free.
4. Revive your Church, O God, bringing a new desire for holiness, righteousness and godliness to your people, and the power of the Holy Spirit as a consequence.
5. Use us daily, O Lord, to bring the Gospel of the forgiveness of sins through Christ to the needy world around about us.

 1 Peter 3:1-7 (1)
True beauty

1. Lord, help us "submit to one another out of reverence for Christ".
2. Let our lives be living testimonies of the beauty of the new life we have in Christ, we pray.
3. Teach us to value the treasures we store up in Heaven more than those we store up on earth, O God.
4. In our dealings with one another, may your grace enable us to be considerate to all, O Lord.
5. Lord, let no action, thought, attitude, decision or anything else we do, hinder our prayers; rather, reveal to us any such hindrance that we may deal with it, we pray.

28th 1 Peter 3:1-7 (2)
Husbands and wives

1. Lord, we bring all the husbands in the church to you. May they love their wives as Christ loved the Church, and gave himself up for her.
2. We ask that your Spirit will move continually upon the fathers, that they may be good, practical and spiritual role models for their sons and daughters.
3. We bring all the wives in the church to you. May they respect their husbands, and may harmony be maintained in each home.
4. We pray for all the mothers in the church that, by their own godly lifestyle, they will influence their children to walk in the ways of the Lord.
5. We pray for the marriages of all those in the church, that you would make them ever stronger, as each couple desires to build their relationship on solid biblical foundations.

29th 1 Peter 3:8-14
Living as ambassadors of Christ

1. Heavenly Father, teach us to live in harmony with each other, and to be quickly reconciled when problems occur.
2. Help us to be compassionate, with understanding hearts and listening ears to those in need or distress.
3. Cause us to remember that it is for you to avenge, O God, not us. Teach us to have forgiving hearts.
4. Lord, right now, we bless all those who have done us wrong. We forgive and release them from our resentment.
5. Cause us to live, in every situation, as an ambassador for the King of all kings.

30th 1 Peter 3:15-17
Always prepared to give an answer

1. Give us courage, O Lord, to always speak out for you when it is necessary.
2. As we read your Word, help us understand and remember, so we can be prepared to answer people with godly wisdom.
3. Holy Spirit, guide our thoughts and words in all situations when we are speaking to others about Jesus.
4. Keep us from error and from straying from the truth of your Word, O Lord.
5. Make us effective witnesses for Jesus, both in our words and in our deeds.

31st 1 Peter 3:18-22
Preaching to the disobedient

1. May we always remember, O Lord, that we were once in darkness, so that we may never forget the plight of those who do not yet know you.
2. May your people never be discouraged by those who reject their witnessing about Jesus, as only you know what a person is truly thinking.
3. Help us to remember that it is the Holy Spirit who causes people to be saved, not us, and that our responsibility is to continue to speak the truth of the Gospel.
4. We pray for all those we know who openly reject Christ. Deal with them as you dealt with Saul of Tarsus, O Lord, and cause them to have a revelation of Jesus.
5. Have mercy on our nation, and pour out your Spirit in saving power, O God.

66 Holy Spirit, strengthen our
will, so that we can exercise
self-control in all areas of our lives,
thoughts and actions,
words and attitudes. **99**

(September 18)

September

Maintaining Righteousness in a Corrupt World

1 Peter Chapters 4 to 5
2 Peter Chapters 1 to 3

During this month, we complete the first of Peter's letters and continue with his second letter, which was written not long after his first. By now, Peter has realised he does not have long left to live, and that he will soon depart this life just as Jesus had prophesied many years earlier, as recorded in John 21:18-19. Peter makes reference to his impending death in 2 Peter 1:14-15.

He recalls in 2 Peter 1:16-18, and takes courage from, his memory of the time on the Mount of Transfiguration, when he saw Jesus in all his divine glory (Mark 9:2-10). Peter looks beyond the suffering he is about to endure, to focus on where he is going and with whom he is going to be. The thoughts of the glory to come give him the strength to press on till the end. In the remaining time he has before he is finally crucified, Peter wants to urge the churches, likewise, to hold on firmly to the faith.

Peter wants to urge the churches, likewise, to hold on firmly to the faith

God will be patient with a wicked world, but the Day of Judgment is certain

What is written in the Bible are not stories invented by clever people, but words inspired by the Holy Spirit, who moved on prophets who wrote them down, just as God breathed them out.

Peter could see prophetically that trouble was coming to the Church and to the world. False teachers would infiltrate the Church and would preach a message corrupted by the ways of the world. Some believers would fall away and go back to the world, just as a pig, once washed, returns back to the mud. Men would mock the idea of the Second Coming of Christ and the preaching of judgment to come. God will be patient with a wicked world, seeking as many as possible to repent and be saved, but the Day of Judgment is certain. So, too, will be the end of this world's ungodly system. Peter reminds us that God will one day create a new Heaven and a new earth, where his Church will live forever in the very presence of God himself.

So, despite any present troubles and trials in this world and lifetime, the future of those who belong to Christ is unspeakably glorious. So we, the Church, should look forward to our destination and our destiny, and make every effort, whilst living in a corrupt world, to live wholly for Christ and his righteousness.

• • • • • • • • • • • • • • • • • •

1st 1 Peter 4:1
Having the same attitude as Christ

1. Lord, help us to become more and more like Jesus.
2. When we are prone to being proud, help us to become more like Jesus.
3. In times when we are tending to act selfishly, help us to become more like Jesus.

4. When our anger is unrighteous rather than righteous, help us to become more like Jesus.
5. When our words would have the effect of being hurtful rather than helpful, unedifying rather than edifying, help us to become more like Jesus.

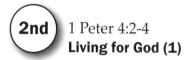 **2nd** 1 Peter 4:2-4
Living for God (1)

1. Cause us to remember, O God, that we have but one life and that it is short. May we each use it as you desire us to.
2. May we truly live out your Word that says, "Those who belong to Christ Jesus have crucified the sinful nature with its passions and desires."
3. Show each of us your will for our lives, O Lord, and give us the grace to seek to fulfil it completely.
4. We pray for those we know in your church, who are struggling with sin or a sinful lifestyle. Help them to make the choice to break free.
5. Show us every hindrance in our lives of our own making, that is preventing us from living fully for you, O Lord.

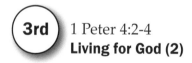 **3rd** 1 Peter 4:2-4
Living for God (2)

1. We pray for those we know, who are in bondage to alcohol, nicotine or drugs. May they turn to you and find complete deliverance, Lord.
2. Help us to make a stand for righteousness when we are put under pressure by non-believers to conform to their ways.
3. When we are mocked or abused for not joining in with the ways of the world, give us your strength and grace to stand, O Lord.
4. Help each of your people in their places of work, when maintaining godly ways and principles puts them under pressure.

5. Help each of your people to maintain godliness in every relationship.

4th 1 Peter 4:5-6
The Day of Reckoning

1. Remembering that one day we will each give an account of our Christian lives to you, Lord Jesus, may we live each hour, each day, each week and each year for you.
2. Wake up every person in your church, O Lord; set us on fire, and help us to fulfil the plan you have for us individually and as a church.
3. Knowing that there is a hell as well as a Heaven, give us a passion for the lost; a passion to intercede, and a passion to win them for Christ.
4. Holy Spirit, reveal to us your strategies for evangelism, both for us as individuals, and for us collectively as your church, that we may be effective soul-winners for Jesus.
5. O God, by your Spirit, help us 'to plunder hell and populate Heaven'.

5th 1 Peter 4:7
The end is near

1. Teach us to number our days, O Lord, and not to waste our time in unprofitable ways.
2. Keep our eyes fixed on Jesus, the Author and Perfecter of our faith, so that we may run the race of life, throwing off everything that hinders.
3. May we be naturally spiritual and spiritually natural, being able to live in the world without being of the world.
4. Help us to redeem the time, making the most of each opportunity, for the days are evil.
5. Let your Kingdom come and your will be done on earth as it is in Heaven.

6th 1 Peter 4:8
Love covers a multitude of sins

1. Lord, may we each make that personal decision to love you with all our being.
2. May we make that personal decision to love each brother and sister in Christ, and each neighbour as ourselves.
3. May we never forget that your love, O Lord, has ensured that all our sins are washed away by the blood of Jesus, and may we love as you have loved us.
4. In our homes, amongst our family members, help us to remember that love covers a multitude of sins.
5. In the church and in the world where we live and work, keep in the forefront of our minds that you desire us always to demonstrate the love of Christ.

7th 1 Peter 4:9
Offer hospitality without grumbling

1. Thank you for our homes, Lord, whether they are grand or humble, for the roof over our heads where we can sleep in peace at night.
2. We pray for all those who are homeless in our community, and for the teams who work in the soup kitchens who reach out to them. Let Jesus be seen and found amongst them.
3. We pray for every home that is opened for meetings and Discipleship Cells. Let your presence, peace and your joy be permanently found in those places.
4. Holy Spirit, as you continue to work in our lives, remove all selfish thoughts and ways from our lives.
5. When we are prone to grumble, help us to stop and speak a blessing instead.

8th 1 Peter 4:10
Using God's gifts

1. Lord, you have given each of us a gift or gifts. Show us our gifts, so we may use them to administer your grace in its various forms.
2. Multiply within your church all the practical gifts that are needed.
3. Multiply within your church all the charismatic gifts that are needed, and baptise all in the Holy Spirit who have not yet been baptised.
4. Help us to see our gifts, not to enhance our own reputations, but as the means to serve others.
5. Thank God for the gift of Jesus. May we bring the gift of salvation in Christ to many, as we use all the various gifts God has given us.

9th 1 Peter 4:11
Bringing praise to God

1. May the words of our mouths and the meditation of our hearts be pleasing in your sight, O Lord.
2. Teach us to speak unto others as we would have them speak unto us; to speak the truth but to speak it in love.
3. Lord, may we measure the words that we speak, so that they are words that you would always be pleased to hear.
4. May our lives be living testimonies to the work of your grace within us, and may the light of Jesus shine out from us at all times and in all situations.
5. Though there are times when we feel we let you down, O Lord, nevertheless, be glorified in each of us, in your church and in our worship.

 1 Peter 4:12-13
Painful trials

1. Help us to remember, Lord, that you have said that in this world we will have trouble, but we can take heart, for you have overcome the world.
2. We pray for those amongst us who are suffering in their family lives. Give them the strength and comfort they need at this time, O Lord.
3. We pray for those who are having trials related to their work situation, or through lack of work. Give them your peace and change their circumstances, O God.
4. We pray for all those who are sick amongst us with long-term sicknesses. Draw near to them in their trial, and may they know your presence and your healing touch.
5. We pray for all those we know or know about, who are suffering for their faith in Christ. Forgive their tormentors, and help your people in their time of need , O Lord.

 1 Peter 4:14-19
Participating in Christ's sufferings

1. Lord, help us to pray with the apostle Paul, "I want to know Christ and the power of his resurrection, and the fellowship of sharing in his sufferings, becoming like him."
2. Lord, help us not simply to choose the easy life or easy way, but always to choose the ways of Christ, even if that leads to trials and suffering.
3. In everything that happens to us, may we live out the belief that you will work all things, including every trial, together for good to those who love you.
4. Lord, your judgment begins with the family of God. May we receive and respond to your discipline in a way that makes us stronger and more effective servants of Jesus.

5. We pray for all those we know, who are suffering times of trial. Give them grace in their time of need, and help them not to be tempted beyond what they can bear.

12th 1 Peter 5:1-4
Elders

1. We pray for our pastors and elders, that you would help them to be everything you desire them to be, O Lord.
2. Give them wisdom in all areas of life, both inside the church and outside.
3. Help each person in a place of leadership or authority in your church to use their position to serve the body of Christ with all effectiveness.
4. Help all those in positions of leadership and authority in the church to be good examples and role models to others, who will, in turn, grow into positions of leadership and authority themselves.
5. Help us to lift up one another's arms as we serve God together and, in particular, those who lead us, so that they may not faint or grow weary with the responsibilities they carry.

13th 1 Peter 5:5-7
The pathway of humility

1. Help us realise, O Lord, that we are nothing and have nothing outside of Christ.
2. We pray for all our youth, that all would take on the mantle of respect for all those who are older.
3. Lord, give us the grace for each of us to treat one another with the humility that is taught in your Word.
4. O God, for all who are prepared to humble themselves under your mighty hand, lift them up to places of great authority and power in Christ.

5. We bring all our cares to you now and lay them at your feet. Help us to trust you to deal with them all.

14th 1 Peter 5:8-9
Resisting the devil

1. O God, give us the strength and wisdom to resist the devil at all times.
2. Let us not give the devil a foothold or toehold into any part of our lives.
3. Give us discernment so that we are not unaware or ignorant of satan's schemes and devices.
4. Help us to use the weapons of spiritual warfare effectively, since they are not the weapons of the world, but ones which have divine power to demolish spiritual strongholds.
5. Keep us strong in our faith, O Lord, no matter what trial or problem may beset us.

15th 1 Peter 5:10-14
Becoming strong in Christ

1. We pray for all those who have been flagging in their faith because of trials; restore them and make them strong, O God.
2. Help us to put suffering into its proper perspective: that it is just a moment in time compared to the eternity of perfect joy we will share with Christ.
3. Cause us to remember to put on the full spiritual armour that you have given to us, so that every flaming arrow of the evil one sent against us will be extinguished.
4. Help us always to stand fast in God, no matter what circumstance we may be going through.
5. May the peace of God, which transcends all understanding, guard our hearts and minds in Christ Jesus.

16th 2 Peter 1:1-2
A precious faith

1. Thank you, Heavenly Father, for the righteousness that comes to us through our faith in Jesus Christ. May we guard it carefully in our lives.
2. We pray for all those we know, whose faith is weak at this time, or is under great pressure. May our words of encouragement help to lift them up.
3. Lord, help us not to trust in our own strength and abilities, but always to trust in you and commit our ways to you, in any and every situation.
4. We believe, Lord, but help us in those times of unbelief that we may go through when the pressure is great.
5. Refine our faith. Cause it to deepen and to grow, so that nothing can shake it.

17th 2 Peter 1:3-4
Precious promises

1. Thank you for your promise that you will never leave us nor forsake us. Cause us to remember that you are watching all we think, say and do.
2. Thank you for your promise that whoever believes in Christ will not perish but have eternal life. May it give us strength, and may it spur us on to share the Good News with others.
3. Thank you for your promise that you, Lord Jesus, are the Resurrection and the Life. We pray for all we know who fear death. May your perfect love cast out all fear.
4. Thank you for your promise that you are the Way, the Truth and the Life. May we allow you to lead us ever deeper into the Father's presence to change us.
5. Thank you for your promise that whoever believes in Jesus, out of his or her innermost being will flow streams of living water. May the Holy Spirit flow out of us more and more.

18th 2 Peter 1:5-9
Growing in the character of Christ

1. Lord, help us to add to our faith the outworking of goodness in our lives.
2. Give us the self-discipline to seek knowledge from your Word, and to grow further spiritually as a result.
3. Holy Spirit, strengthen our will, so that we can exercise self-control in all areas of our lives, thoughts and actions, words and attitudes.
4. Give us the grace never to give up, but to persevere in all things that are godly.
5. Increase in our midst brotherly and sisterly kindness, and the *agapé* love of God one to another.

 19th 2 Peter 1:10-11
Making our calling sure

1. Lord, keep us from backsliding, even for a day.
2. We pray for all those we know, who are struggling in their faith and are backsliding. Bring them back to a close relationship with you, we pray.
3. We pray for all our family members and friends who once walked strongly with you but are not doing so now. Move on them to have the desire to turn back to you, O Lord.
4. When we are tempted to give up or turn back, help us to keep our eyes fixed on the rich welcome we will receive into the eternal Kingdom of our Lord and Saviour, Jesus Christ.
5. Help us to keep in proper perspective and contrast, the temporary riches of the world and the eternal riches of the Kingdom of Christ.

2 Peter 1:12-15
Remember these truths

1. Lord, as we start each day, help us to let our thoughts dwell on the indescribable blessings that are ours in Christ Jesus.
2. Thank you, Lord, for the sure and certain knowledge that the moment we die, we shall be immediately welcomed into the glorious presence of God.
3. We bless you, Lord, for the sure and certain knowledge that we will be given new, resurrected bodies that will never grow old or sick.
4. Thank you, Lord, that we are new creations in Christ; the old has gone and the new has come. May we conduct ourselves as befits our new status.
5. Lord, we remember with joy and excitement your death and resurrection, your ascension, and your sending forth the Holy Spirit into our lives.

 2 Peter 1:16-18
Not cleverly-invented stories

1. Lord, your Word is the Word of God. Help us not to live by bread alone, but by every Word of God.
2. For all those we know, who struggle with doubts concerning the promises in your Word, strengthen their faith, we pray.
3. Give us the wisdom to use your Word carefully and accurately when we are talking with non-Christians.
4. We pray for all those Christians who are confused in their faith, because of the teachings of the Theory of Evolution. Give them clarity of mind and understanding.
5. Help us to build our lives fully and completely on the bedrock of your Word, O Lord, and not on the shifting sands of man's opinions.

2 Peter 1:19-21
Prophecy

1. Thank you, Holy Spirit, that you speak to men and women today. Speak to us and give us minds to understand what you are saying to us.
2. Holy Spirit, speak to us as a church, and may we follow your leading in every area of the life of the church.
3. Increase the gift of prophecy amongst us, so that we use the gift to strengthen, encourage and comfort men and women.
4. Today, Holy Spirit, fill us afresh to overflowing, so that you may flow out of us into the lives of those around us.
5. Holy Spirit, give us a fresh vision of Jesus and the work of the cross that will renew and revive our dedication to Christ and the work of God.

2 Peter 2:1-3
False prophets and false teachers

1. Lord, we pray that you will keep us from all forms of heresy and false teaching.
2. Holy Spirit, help us to keep close to Jesus, so that our minds do not become infected with falsehood in any form.
3. Lord, give us the discernment to be able to distinguish truth from error, so that we may not go astray.
4. Since satan can appear as an angel of light, guard us in all temptations, so that we are not deceived by sin that is disguised or hidden.
5. We pray for all those who preach and teach in the church and in the Discipleship Cells or any other class, that each would speak the truth, the whole truth and nothing but the truth of God's Word.

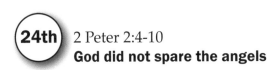

24th 2 Peter 2:4-10
God did not spare the angels

1. Lord, cause us always to remember that you are a God of righteous judgment as well as a God of love, so that we will always walk in reverence before you.
2. Lord, we pray for the communities we live in, that you would move in saving power to bring them into your Kingdom before it is too late.
3. Have mercy on those we know who are as yet unsaved, O Lord, and in your great love, cause them to recognise their need of you and repent of their sins.
4. Lord, may the certain knowledge of a Day of Judgment that is coming spur us on to reach the lost.
5. Have mercy on our nation, O Lord, that is systematically revoking our nation's laws that were once based on your Word, and turn our nation back to you.

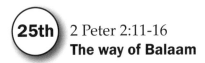

25th 2 Peter 2:11-16
The way of Balaam

1. Lord, Balaam sinned by turning to the occult. Forgive any of us who have once been involved with any form of fortune telling or contacting spirits, and we renounce such contacts right now.
2. Lord, we renounce right now anything in our lives that has become idolatrous worship, and turn away completely from it.
3. As Balaam loved money more than obedience to you, O Lord, forgive us when we have fallen into the same error.
4. Lord, may we never covet anything you have not given us, except the gifts of the Holy Spirit, which you have told us to "covet earnestly".
5. Lord, keep us from rebellion against your ways, even if it is only in small ways, and forgive us when we have done so.

26th 2 Peter 2:17-22
Becoming entangled again in the corruption of the world

1. Having put our hands to the plough, O Lord, may we never be tempted to look back again.
2. We pray for all those we know, who have once walked with the Lord, but who have turned back to the way of the world. Have mercy and restore them, we pray.
3. We pray for those who, because of times of trial, are being tempted to return to the ways of the world. Give them the courage and strength to say "No" to sin.
4. For every 'prodigal son or daughter' who hears the cries of their mother and father, let the parents have the joy of seeing their prodigals return to Christ.
5. We pray over your church, O Lord, that the ways of the world would not be allowed - through neither the front door nor the back door - into the life of the church.

27th 2 Peter 3:1-7
Scoffers

1. When people ridicule our faith in Christ, give each of us your strength and grace to stand and to pray for those who mock.
2. Help us to discern which of those, who seem to be against Christ, are really like Saul of Tarsus, that is, ready for a dramatic conversion.
3. We pray for all our youth and children, that they will not be influenced in their faith by scoffers in the educational system.
4. Give us a heart of pity and not anger, for those who scoff at the claims of Christ, since we know their destiny if they refuse to turn from their sin.
5. Lord, though we are saved from your wrath on the Day of Judgment, let us not be complacent but earnestly work while it is still day.

28th 2 Peter 3:8-9
A day is as a thousand years

1. Lord, help us to see time from your perspective, so that we do not grow weary and give up.
2. Give us patience when we are undergoing those times of trial that seem to be so long, and to remember that you work all things together for the good of those who love you.
3. Help us in the time still remaining before your return, O Lord, to use this time of your patience to reach many of the lost for Christ.
4. May the expectation and anticipation of spending eternity in your glorious presence keep us joyful in every circumstance of our present lives here on earth.
5. Thank you, Lord, that you always keep your promises, and your delays are always for a good reason. Help us never to waiver, whilst we wait for the fulfilment of your promises.

29th 2 Peter 3:10–13
Like a thief

1. Lord, help us not to be like the five foolish virgins, but to remain alert and keep watch, because we do not know the hour.
2. Whilst we wait for your return, Lord Jesus, may we use the talents you have given us to produce lasting fruit for your Kingdom.
3. Lord, help us to discern the times and the seasons of your return, so that we may not be ashamed at the Day of your coming.
4. Empower us daily so you can build your Church through us, that the gates of hell will be unable to prevail against it.
5. Even so, come, Lord Jesus!

30th 2 Peter 3:14-18
Do not be carried away by error

1. Holy Spirit, help us to make every effort to be found spotless and blameless and at peace with God.
2. Help us always to be on guard against error, sin, temptation and every other device and trap of the enemy.
3. Help us to remain rooted and grounded in Christ Jesus and in the solid Word of God.
4. Change us, Lord, day by day, so that we continue to grow in the grace of the Lord Jesus Christ.
5. As the moon reflects the light of the sun, may your presence be seen in us and in all we do, so that you may be glorified.

" Strengthen us, your Church,
O God, for the spiritual battles
that lie ahead, as the devil knows
his time is short and seeks to
come more and more
against your people. **"**

(October 12)

October

Working While There is Still Time

Joel 1:1 to 3:21

The message of the prophet Joel shows clearly the two aspects of God's nature. As the righteous and holy Ruler of the universe, God cannot overlook sin; all sin will be punished. This includes the sins of the nations, starting with the people of God.

Joel's prophecies span the whole of time: from the present in his day, down to the end of this current age, when God will bring an end to the current era, and will himself step down from Heaven once again and physically intervene in the affairs of men. The nations of the world will be judged, and Jesus will set up his Kingdom over the whole world, with his headquarters in Jerusalem.

And yet, the other aspect to God's nature that Joel shows is love, and God's preferred option is that people, both as individuals and as nations, rather than having to be judged, would turn from their sins and turn to him in repentance

> **God's preferred option is that people ... would turn from their sins and turn to him in repentance**

God's prophetic clock is ticking, and it is now two minutes to midnight

instead. Then he can pardon them and they can be recipients of all his gracious promises.

Those promises include the pouring out of his Holy Spirit upon young and old, men and women alike, to be able to experience life in the supernatural, even now in this lifetime, operating in the gifts of the Holy Spirit, just as Jesus did when he came to this earth as a man the first time. When Jesus returns for the second time, it will be not as the suffering Servant but as the triumphant King, vanquishing his enemies; judging the nations, and ruling over the earth in righteousness.

There is a limited time. Today is the day of salvation, but it will not last forever. God's prophetic clock is ticking, and it is now two minutes to midnight. Time is short to see people saved. As we pray through the book of Joel, we are praying for the Church and the nations to turn back to God, and for many to get saved while time still remains.

• • • • • • • • • • • • • • • • • • •

 1st Joel 1:1-2
Listening to God's warnings

1. Lord, give us ears to listen when you speak to us as individuals, and help us to discern all that you are saying to us.
2. Help us as a church to know the mind of God, and to fulfil the destiny, plans and purposes you have for us to make a godly impact on our society and nation.
3. We pray for our nation, O Lord, that it will heed the warnings you send, and turn back from its unrighteous ways.
4. Speak to us as individuals, O Lord, that we may hear from you daily, guiding our thoughts, directing our circumstances and ordering our ways.

5. Give us prophetic insight into the things you plan to do, O Lord, that we may always be in tune with what you are doing and with all that you are planning.

2nd Joel 1:3-4
Instructing the next generations

1. Help each parent in the church to raise up their sons and daughters in the instruction of the Lord, we pray.
2. We pray for all our children, that you would cause them to learn and to heed, and to make the Lord the foundation of their lives from their earliest years.
3. We pray for our schools, O Lord, that our children would continue to be taught the Bible, and that attempts to have those lessons removed will be frustrated.
4. We pray for all our Sunday school teachers, that you would give them wisdom and godly influence into the lives of those they teach, and that you would encourage their hearts as they see children responding to God's Word.
5. We pray for all the children in our land, who never get the chance to hear the Word of God or to know the teaching of the Bible; help them to get opportunities to hear and be influenced by your Word, O Lord.

3rd Joel 1:5
The true new wine

1. We pray for the people of our nation, whose lives are so empty and unfulfilled that they find it necessary to find satisfaction in alcohol; lead us to such individuals, and help us direct them to the One who can meet all their deepest needs.
2. Lord, as individuals, may we not be drunk with new wine, but instead be filled with the Spirit of God.

3. We pray for a daily infilling of your Holy Spirit, O Lord, that will enable us to become more and more effective in our service for you.
4. For those of us who are seeking the baptism in the Holy Spirit, fill us now as we wait upon you, O God.
5. Holy Spirit, help us to stir up the fire already within us, and add new spiritual gifts to those within our congregation that may be used for your glory.

4th Joel 1:6-7
Dangers to our nation

1. Lord, open the eyes of your Church to every spiritual danger that is at work within our nation, that we may intercede effectively.
2. We pray for those who govern us, that their eyes would be opened to the spiritual dangers that are now at work in our nation as a result of ungodly decisions in high places.
3. Raise up your intercessors throughout this land, O Lord, who may be able, by the power of prayer, to overcome the dark spiritual forces operating in and over our nation.
4. May your Church not sleep whilst its spiritual enemies are actively seeking its downfall; let your Church awake to the dangers and take decisive action, we pray.
5. Rise up in our midst, O Lord, and let your enemies be scattered.

5th Joel 1:8-9
Mourn over our nation

1. Lord, we bring our nation before you, and pray that you will have mercy upon us for rejecting your laws and implementing new ones that are anathema to you.
2. Have mercy on your Church in this nation, O Lord, for sleeping while the enemy has been working to steal the soul of our nation.

3. Have mercy on those who make the laws in this country, O God, when those laws have saddened your heart.
4. Lord, open the eyes of your Church to the spiritual decline all around us; remove complacency, and put in our spirits the urgency of the dangers, that we may act and pray to bring change.
5. No matter how much wickedness there may now be in our nation, O God, we pray that in your mercy you would forgive and cleanse our land.

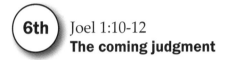

6th Joel 1:10-12
The coming judgment

1. Lord, as your Word instructs us, may we examine ourselves daily, and deal with anything displeasing to you, so that we may not fall under your discipline.
2. For all in your Church, O Lord, who profess to follow you, but whose lives are not consistent with their words, bring them back to a close walk with you.
3. Lord, if there is any hidden sin in your Church that hinders you working amongst us, reveal it, so nothing can prevent you moving in power amongst us.
4. Lord, you are sovereign over all, and are able to humble this nation in a moment; have mercy and turn back the tide of wickedness before it is too late and judgment must fall, we pray.
5. Send revival to our nation, O Lord, so that you will not need to visit this land with judgment.

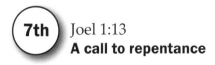

7th Joel 1:13
A call to repentance

1. Lord, may we be the first to heed your call to repentance, that we may always be in right relationship with you.

2. Lord, may each person, who is in a position of leadership, heed your call to repentance and so continually walk humbly before you.
3. Lord, may each person in a place of influence in the Church, heed your call to repentance and walk humbly before you.
4. Lord, we confess the sins of your Church, and ask you to forgive, restore and raise up to power and influence, the people of God in this land - and start with us, we pray.
5. We confess the sins of our nation and all those who lived before us; forgive, we pray, and may this generation be a generation that rises up to bring change for good.

8th Joel 1:14-18
A call to fasting

1. May we take the sin of this nation seriously, O Lord, and not become immune to the ever-increasing ungodliness that surrounds us.
2. Give us a burden not only to mourn the sins of our nation, but also to pray and to fast to seek the face of God for mercy.
3. May our prayer meetings be powerhouses of spiritual dynamite that wreak havoc amongst the powers of darkness in high places, O God.
4. Wake up your Church to the power that there is in prayer, when we truly use this spiritual weapon as you desire us to, O God, and cause us to pray effectively.
5. Raise up men and women like Elijah, O God, who can fast and pray powerful and effective, strategic prayers that have national influence.

9th Joel 1:19-20
Calling out to God

1. Hear our cries, O Lord, and listen to the prayers of your people, as we seek you in spirit and in truth.

2. Though you tarry, O Lord, may we not grow weary in prayer and give up, but rather continue to wrestle to overcome spiritual powers of darkness, and pull down spiritual strongholds.
3. Place on our hearts each day the strategic prayers you would have us to pray, O Lord, so that we do not pray amiss, but perfectly in line with your will.
4. Intervene in the affairs of our nation, O God, and do not let those who reject you or despise you have their way over the people of this land, we pray.
5. As we continue to call out to you to send revival in our land, hear the cries of those interceding, and send a new move of your Holy Spirit in revival power, we pray.

 10th Joel 2:1
Sound the alarm

1. Let your Church rise up the length and breadth of the country, O Lord, to raise the alarm that our nation is sleepwalking to destruction unless it starts to turn back to God.
2. Give us a renewed understanding of sin as you see it, O God, that we may understand the urgency of the hour.
3. We pray for every denomination across our land that, up and down the country, you would bring revival to churches in the cities, towns and villages.
4. May we, your Church, become more vocal in raising the alarm of the sin in our nation and its destructive consequences, and give us influence to bring change, we pray.
5. Give us opportunities daily to speak out for you and your ways, O Lord, and give us the boldness we need to do so.

 11th Joel 2:2-5
The coming battle

1. Lord, you have given us the spiritual weapons to overcome every demonic power at work in our society; give us the insight and desire to use them powerfully and effectively, we pray.

2. Thank you, Lord Jesus, that you have delegated to your Church your power and authority; help us to be able to use it with boldness and effectively, without fear.
3. Lord, your Word is sharper than a double-edged sword, judging thoughts and attitudes of the heart; may we not neglect your Word, but learn to use it effectively.
4. Lord, help us to remove every trace of habitual sin in our lives, so that the devil may not gain a foothold and so overcome us.
5. May the God of peace soon crush satan underneath our feet.

12th Joel 2:6-11
The Day of the Lord

1. Lord, prepare us, your Church, for the present battle against the powers of darkness and the wickedness that already is at work in our society.
2. Lord, as the spirit of antichrist is all around us, we pray that you would equip us to make a stand against all the ungodliness that surrounds us, that we may stand and not fall.
3. Strengthen us, your Church, O God, for the spiritual battles that lie ahead, as the devil knows his time is short and seeks to come more and more against your people.
4. Give us grace, O Lord, to stand in the day of trouble and in times of trial.
5. Come, O Lord Jesus; may your Kingdom come and your will be done here on earth just as it is in Heaven.

13th Joel 2:12
Turn to the Lord

1. Lord, may we turn to you with all our hearts, with nothing in our lives having a priority before you.
2. We pray for all those we know who once walked with the Lord, but who have now backslidden; cause them to repent and turn back to you, we pray.

3. We pray for our Sunday services, and ask that many unsaved people would be drawn to hear your Word and give their lives to you, O God.
4. We pray for all our evangelism, whether as individuals or as a group; help us to lead many people to Christ on the streets, in our homes, and in our places of work, we pray.
5. We pray for all our Discipleship Cells that many would find Christ as their Saviour through the work of the Cells.

 Joel 2:13-14
The power of intercession

1. Lord, give us the burden to pray and then to see the powerful effects of our prayers.
2. We bring all our prayer meetings to you, and ask that you would cause them to overflow with people seeking you in prayer.
3. Raise up more intercessors, who have the burden and the spiritual strategies to move mountains; pull down spiritual strongholds, and defeat every demonic strategy against your church, O Lord.
4. As we seek you in prayer, O God, move amongst us more and more with signs, wonders, miracles and astonishing answers to prayer.
5. Lord, as your people turn to you more and more in prayer, may you encourage our hearts with the blessings that flow as a consequence, we pray.

 Joel 2:15-16
Gather together to seek God

1. Lord, all those of your people, who are too lazy to meet regularly together in church, stir them up and ignite their hearts, we pray.
2. Fill our Sunday services to overflowing, as your people bring the unsaved to hear the life-changing message of the Gospel, O Lord.

3. For all those who feel discouraged and have stopped attending church, touch their hearts once again with your love, O Lord.
4. May our meetings - whether large gatherings or small groups - be anointed and empowered by the Holy Spirit to see Jesus lifted up and glorified in our midst, we pray.
5. Send revival to all our meetings, O Lord, as your people meet together with a deep desire to seek your face and your will.

16th Joel 2:17
Prayer for ministers

1. Lord, we pray for the pastors of our church, that they would continually walk closely with you day by day, overcoming every attack of the evil one.
2. We pray for all our elders, that you would give them wisdom as they govern the church.
3. We pray for all those who function in the role of deacon, in the day-to-day practical affairs of the church, that you would guide and lead them to serve you with all the skill they require, O God.
4. We pray for all those who are leaders of Discipleship Cells, that you would encourage their hearts as they minister weekly into the lives of others.
5. We pray for everyone in the church who is ministering to others, whether teaching or any other kind of ministry; bless them, protect them, and make them effective in all they do.

17th Joel 2:18-20
God's blessing and protection

1. Lord, watch over and keep your people from every circumstance that would bring us down or cause discouragement.
2. Protect your people from every fiery dart and flaming arrow from the evil one, we pray; may the shield of our faith extinguish every such attack.

3. For those amongst us who have been praying for a long time for specific matters, bring breakthroughs now, we pray.
4. Lord, in times of national financial difficulties, we pray you would continue to prosper your people financially.
5. Lord, as your people continually seek you, we pray that your protection would be over every part of our lives at all times.

 18th Joel 2:21-24
Rejoicing in God's intervention and blessings

1. Lord, we thank you for every blessing in our lives and for every answer to prayer; may we continue to be a thankful people.
2. We pray that this may be a season of breakthrough in the spiritual lives of individuals in the church, that will then impact the lives of all those around about them.
3. We pray that this may be a season of spiritual breakthrough in the life of the church, that will take us to a new higher spiritual level.
4. Intervene in the life of our nation, O Lord, and where there is sin, heartache and distress, cause changes in our society that bring blessing instead.
5. Overcome darkness and send spiritual blessings into our nation, O Lord.

 19th Joel 2:25-26
Restoring the years the locusts have eaten

1. Lord, the 'locusts' have eaten away at much of the spiritual life of our nation over the years; restore to us what they have eaten, we pray.
2. Lord, the 'locusts' have eaten away at much of the spiritual life of your Church up and down the land over the years; restore to us what they have eaten.

3. Lord, our society has many problems and ills as a result of what the 'locusts' have eaten; restore peace back to our society once more.
4. For all in our midst, who have been suffering ill-health over the years, restore to them full health and strength in Jesus' Name, we pray.
5. For any of your people, whose lives have been blighted by the actions of others, as they forgive and bless those people, restore to them what they have suffered over the years, we pray.

(20th) Joel 2:27
Knowing God is God

1. Lord, increase our daily walk and experience with you, that we may know you in a deeper way, and that our faith and our effectiveness may grow.
2. Take away all fear from our lives, O Lord, but instead may we rise up in a new anointing of power, strength and effectiveness, we pray.
3. May we daily move in the power of God as part of our normal experience, O Lord.
4. Rise up in power in our midst, O Lord, to save the lost, heal the sick, set the captives free, and to change lives and circumstances.
5. Open the eyes of those who worship other gods, and enable us to lead them to a knowledge of the true and living God, we pray.

(21st) Joel 2:28-29 (1)
Pouring out his Spirit

1. Lord, increase within us a spiritual hunger for more of the things of the Holy Spirit in every part of our lives.
2. For those amongst us who have not yet been baptised in the Holy Spirit and are seeking, fill them now, we pray.
3. Sweep through all our young men and women, and fill them with your Holy Spirit, O Lord.

4. Touch all our older people, O God, and manifest amongst them more strategic and prophetic dreams and visions.

5. Let the whole church come alive in the presence of your Holy Spirit, O God, that we may be led, guided and instructed by the Spirit of the Lord.

22nd Joel 2:28-29 (2)
Spiritual gifts

1. Pour out the gift of speaking in tongues upon us, O Lord, and may we use the gift to enhance our devotional lives and draw closer to you.

2. Pour out amongst us the gifts of the interpretation of messages in tongues and the gift of prophecy, we pray.

3. Endow us with the gifts of words of knowledge and words of wisdom, especially in the evangelistic setting, where they may be used to bring unbelievers to Christ.

4. We pray for an increased operation of the gifts of healings and of miracles, that would cause the unsaved to acknowledge the truth of the Gospel, and of Jesus as Saviour.

5. We pray for the gifts of discerning of spirits, that would help us defeat the powers of darkness, and the gift of faith that moves mountains.

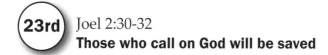

23rd Joel 2:30-32
Those who call on God will be saved

1. Lord, we pray for a new move of God that will enable us to see countless people turn to Christ and get saved.

2. Holy Spirit, we ask that when we witness to the unsaved or preach, that you would bring a great conviction in their hearts, and they would desire to be saved.

3. Lead us to those who are ready to be saved, O Lord, and open the eyes of the spiritually blind.

4. We pray for all our services where the Gospel is preached, that we would always see the unsaved responding and giving their lives to Christ.
5. We pray for every unsaved person we speak to about Christ, whether at work, on the streets or at home, that you, Holy Spirit, would cause them to be convicted of sin, and call to God for salvation.

24th Joel 3:1-3
Judgment on the nations

1. We pray for all the nations of Europe, O Lord, that you would have mercy upon them, and cause their populations to turn to Christ.
2. We pray for all the nations of Africa, O Lord; bring many more to Christ before time runs out.
3. We pray for all the nations in Asia; in these last days, send revivals to those countries that have never yet experienced such a move of God.
4. We pray for North and South America, that you would spread revival from Canada's Arctic North to Argentina's Tierra del Fuego in the deep south.
5. Send revival to Australasia and to all the island nations around the world before it is too late, O Lord.

25th Joel 3:4-9
Praying for nations hostile to the Lord (1)

1. Lord, we pray for all the Muslim nations; open their eyes to the deity of Christ, save them and send revival to them, we pray.
2. Lord, we pray for the Hindu nations, that you would open their eyes to the fact that there is but one true God, and turn them to Christ, we pray.

3. We pray for the Buddhist nations; cause them to stop trusting in salvation by works, and cause them to trust in Christ by faith alone.

4. We pray for the Communist nations; reveal to them the reality of God, Heaven and hell, and cause them to turn to Christ, we pray.

5. We pray for the Jews who have not accepted Christ as their promised Messiah; open their eyes to the truth, and cause them to read the Old Testament with renewed vision and understanding, O Lord.

 26th Joel 3:10-13
Praying for the nations hostile to the Lord (2)

1. We pray for those nations led by military dictatorships that persecute Christians; save them, O Lord, through the heroic witness of your people.

2. We pray for all your people who are persecuted simply for believing in Christ; let them sense the closeness of your presence in the midst of their trials, O Lord.

3. We pray for all those who convert to Christ from other religions, and whose lives are in danger as a consequence; do not let the fear of man hinder countless people turning to Christ in this way, O Lord.

4. We pray for all your people who are currently in prisons or labour camps, simply because they follow Christ; strengthen and comfort their hearts in their trials, O God.

5. We pray for the democratic nations, including our own, that are increasingly marginalising true believers through laws that oppose biblical values; help your Church to prevail and rise up stronger, despite such attacks, O God.

27th Joel 3:14-16
Multitudes heading for destruction

1. We pray for all our unsaved family members; save them, O Lord.
2. We pray for all those in our places of work who are unsaved; help our witness, through actions and words, cause them to accept Christ, O God.
3. We pray for all those we meet on the streets and who receive tracts; convict them as we speak, and help us lead them to Christ, O Lord.
4. We pray for all those who attend our church services, but who have never made a personal commitment to Christ; convict them and save them now, O God.
5. Lord, as we are in the last days, send a great revival in our midst, and use us to lead many to Christ in these days, O Lord.

28th Joel 3:17
The peace of Jerusalem

1. Lord, as your Word instructs us, we continue to pray for the peace of Jerusalem.
2. Come, Lord Jesus, we pray, and take your rightful place as King over this world, with your headquarters in Jerusalem.
3. Lord, we pray for the land of Israel, that you would quicken the pace at which Jews are realising that Jesus is indeed their promised Messiah and are accepting him as Saviour.
4. Lord, we pray for all the Palestinians in Jerusalem and in Israel, that you would cause many more of them to come to know and accept Christ as their personal Saviour.
5. Give wisdom to those who lead the Israeli government in Jerusalem, O Lord, and may your perfect will be done there.

29th Joel 3:18
God's provision

1. Lord, you are the great Provider; we pray that you would meet each of our needs as they arise.
2. Meet all the spiritual needs of our nation and of the society in which we live, we pray; fill the nation's spiritual vacuum with Christ.
3. For all who need jobs at this time and are seeking your help, meet their needs and provide, we pray.
4. For all who are setting up businesses and are seeking your help in such ventures, guide them and provide for their every need, we pray.
5. When you provide for us and bless us financially, O Lord, may we not just keep it all for ourselves, but rather be generous to bless your work and others, too.

30th Joel 3:19-21
God's pardon (1)

1. Lord, pardon our national leaders for their sin of turning away from you, we pray.
2. Lord, pardon our local government leaders for their sin of turning away from you, we pray.
3. Lord, pardon those who run our national institutions for their sin of turning away from you.
4. Lord, pardon all the church leaders who have sinned by compromising with worldly ways and ideas, and so have turned away from you.
5. Lord, have mercy on all church members who have sinned by compromising with the ways of this world, and so have turned away from you.

(31st) Joel 3:19-21
God's pardon (2)

1. Lord, pardon your Church for those times when we have lacked zeal, and re-ignite us, we pray.
2. Lord, pardon your Church when we have allowed other, less important things to have precedence over our relationship with you; renew our love, we pray.
3. Lord, pardon your Church when we have kept silent when we should have spoken out; give us boldness, we pray.
4. Lord, forgive your Church when we have compromised rather than standing firm; give us wisdom and courage, we pray.
5. Lord, forgive your Church when we have failed to love you with all our heart, mind, strength and soul, and our neighbours as ourselves; change us into your image, we pray.

November

Practical Holiness
Leviticus Chapter 19:1-37

The Christian life is not blind obedience to a set of external rules and regulations, but rather living in personal relationship with a holy God. As a consequence of inviting this holy God into our lives through repentance and faith in Jesus Christ, we are changed from the inside out, being led of God's Holy Spirit, who is now within us and enabling us to follow God's ways through our own desire to obey, which becomes instinctive.

When we begin this new relationship with God through faith in Christ and are, in Jesus' words, 'born again' and are now adopted into God's family, the Bible tells us that we are 'sanctified', that is, set apart; set apart from our old way of life, and set apart to follow the new way of life that is God's way. Another way of describing this is being 'holy'.

Many people measure themselves against others, using the measurement of being 'good'. So they may say, "I am as good as the next person. I am as good as those who go to church.

The Christian life is not blind obedience to a set of external rules and regulations

> ## God doesn't call people to a life of trying to be 'good'... he commands, "Be holy, for I am holy"

I do more good things than bad." But since, "all have sinned and fall short of the glory of God" (Romans 3:23), being 'good' is not good enough. God doesn't call people to a life of trying to be 'good'. That would fall infinitely short of his righteous standards. Rather, he commands, "Be holy, for I am holy" (Leviticus 19:2). And his Word clearly states that, "Without holiness no-one will see the Lord" (Hebrews 12:14). No-one can begin to live a life of holiness unless they have Christ and the power of the Holy Spirit working within them.

So, what does practical holiness look like?

It is living and working in a fallen world, and yet always conforming to the higher standards in every area of our lives that God calls us to. It relates to our actions, attitudes, thoughts and behaviour in all the situations, matters and circumstances we have to deal with on a day-to-day basis. The Book of Leviticus is a book that sets out areas of practical holiness. Whilst some parts relate to the ceremonial law, which Christ fulfilled on our behalf (such as the sacrifices), others describe some very practical ways by which God wants us to live out a life of holiness, in ways which have never changed.

A biblical principle which runs throughout the Book of Leviticus is: be a clean people.

Practical holiness here is seen to include a clean body, clean clothes, clean houses kept free from damp and mildew, and clean morals kept free from sexual misuse. And here in Chapter 19, it includes how we relate to one another; treat one another; show respect to one another, and to God. This is how the Holy Spirit wants to lead us.

• • • • • • • • • • • • • • • • • •

1st Leviticus 19:1-2
Be holy, because I am holy

1. Lord, help us to live as ones who are set apart to live, not according to the world's ways, but according to your ways.
2. Help us, O Lord, to live our lives as ones who are in this world but not of this world, being naturally spiritual and spiritually natural.
3. May the words of our mouths be holy unto you, O God.
4. May the intents of our hearts, and the actions we do, be holy in your sight, O Lord.
5. May our bodies be offered unto you, O Lord, as living sacrifices, holy and pleasing to you.

 2nd Leviticus 19:3
Respect

1. We pray that the importance of the family, as the bedrock of society, will be acknowledged, and that our Government will take measures to defend and strengthen the family.
2. Teach us to be a people who show proper respect to our parents, honouring them if they are following Christ, and praying for their salvation if they do not know Christ.
3. Teach us to live our lives in a way that always shows respect to you, O God, as our Heavenly Father.
4. May we order our lives and our affairs in a way that ensures we can join in the corporate worship each week, and for those who struggle in this area, help them find a way, we pray.
5. We pray for our nation, that respect for you, O Lord, and for our weekly day of worship, will be restored once more to our society.

3rd Leviticus 19:4
True worship

1. If we have anything in our lives that we treat as a greater priority than you, and so has become an idol, O Lord, convict us and enable us now to remove it.
2. Strengthen us, O God, to be able to love you with all our heart, soul, strength and mind.
3. Turn our nation away from idolatry in all its forms, and turn it back to you, O God.
4. We pray for all those in our nation, who are worshipping false gods; reveal yourself to them, O Lord, that they may know the joy of worshipping the true God.
5. We pray for all those in our nation who worship nothing truly spiritual, but live only for themselves; open their eyes, and save them before it is too late for them, we pray.

4th Leviticus 19:5-8
Acceptable sacrifice

1. May the spiritual sacrifices that we offer up to you, O Lord, be made from a pure heart and so be acceptable to you.
2. May our prayers come up to you from sincere motives, and so be acceptable to you, O God.
3. May our songs of worship come up to you with the sole desire to bring you praise and glory, and so be acceptable to you, O Lord.
4. May our works of service be done for you with the motive purely of love for you and for others, so they will be acceptable to you, O Lord.
5. May our lives be such, O God, that one day we will hear your words, "Well done, good and faithful servant."

 **5th** Leviticus 19:9-10
Generosity

1. Teach us to be a people who are not afraid to be generous givers, O Lord.
2. May we never be afraid to give to you, O God, with our tithes and offerings.
3. Lead us to those people you want us to bless by helping them with our time and labour, or by giving them something financially.
4. May we know the joy of giving, and the truth of your words, O Lord, "It is more blessed to give than to receive."
5. Teach us to be a people who give, whether our time, effort or finances, out of love and not out of duty.

 **6th** Leviticus 19:11 (1)
Honesty

1. Lord, let us be a people who can always be trusted in all things, and especially as a witness before the unsaved.
2. Cause us to remember your words, "Whoever can be trusted with very little can also be trusted with much," and so be people who are trustworthy in even the smallest details.
3. As employees in our places of work, may we be diligent, careful not to 'steal' our employers' time by not working faithfully.
4. Help us always to be careful stewards of money, especially if it is somebody else's.
5. May we not 'steal' your time, O Lord, by neglecting the time we need to spend in your presence.

7th Leviticus 19:11 (2)
Truthfulness

1. Keep our lips from speaking falsehood, O Lord.
2. Let us be people whose word is our bond, and whose "Yes" is "Yes," and whose "No" is "No."
3. Teach us, O Lord, that even if we cannot see how, you will always honour us if we choose to do things your way, and we will never need to resort to deceit.
4. You have called us to walk in your ways and, as God, you never lie; help us to be like you in all we do.
5. Forgive us, O God, for the times we have spoken untruthfully; give us the integrity and strength not to repeat our mistakes.

8th Leviticus 19:12
Taking God's Name in vain

1. Let us be a people, O Lord, who never make promises we do not keep.
2. Help us to keep our word - even when it hurts.
3. May we not use your Name in a frivolous way, but always be mindful that you are God Almighty.
4. Thank you, O Lord, that you have delegated to us, as your Church, the authority of your Name; may we use your Name righteously, powerfully and effectively, O Lord.
5. The Name of the Lord is a strong tower; may we continually walk in the ways of righteousness, so we can be safe.

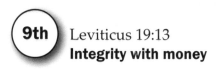

9th Leviticus 19:13
Integrity with money

1. In all our dealings with money, may we always be careful to act with the utmost integrity, we pray.

2. If we owe any person any money, make us to be people who are careful to pay it back as and when we have promised to do so, O Lord.
3. May our testimony not be compromised by any lack of integrity on our part regarding how we handle money, we pray.
4. Help us keep up our guard, so that the devil is not able to gain a foothold into our lives through our careless handling of money.
5. Give us hearts that are generous and not penny-pinching, we pray.

 10th Leviticus 19:14
Kindness towards the less fortunate

1. Give us compassionate hearts towards those who are less fortunate than ourselves, O Lord.
2. We pray for all those we know, who have physical disabilities in one way or another; bless them, and meet all their needs, we pray.
3. We pray for all those we know, who are suffering mentally or emotionally; bless them, and help them to full healing of their minds and hearts, we pray.
4. We pray that we would see the ever-increasing evidence of the power of God in our midst, to bring healing in every area of body, mind and emotions, we pray.
5. Teach us to be grateful for all the blessings in our lives, O Lord, so that we do not complain against you.

 11th Leviticus 19:15
Fairness

1. In any area where we lack wisdom, O Lord, we ask that you would give us your divine wisdom in all matters.
2. Give us wisdom in our dealings with fellow believers, to ensure we always deal with one another fairly and in a godly fashion, we pray.

3. Give us the wisdom in our dealings with those in the world who are unbelievers, that we may always deal with them in a way that is fair and righteous, O God.
4. Give us eyes that look upon all people, no matter who they are, as equally deserving of our Christian love, we pray, even if we need to rebuke them.
5. Give us the discernment, O Lord, to know how to settle disputes that we may find ourselves involved with, in a way that is pleasing to you.

12th Leviticus 19:16
No harm to someone's character or person

1. Keep our lips from gossip, O Lord.
2. Keep our hearts from running down a person's character, even if they have not behaved well; instead, leaving you to let them reap for themselves what they may have sown.
3. So far as it is depends upon us, O God, enable us to live at peace with everyone.
4. Let us be people who are not overcome by evil, but rather who overcome evil with good.
5. Enable us to be careful in all our daily actions, so that we do nothing that would carelessly bring harm to someone else.

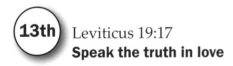

13th Leviticus 19:17
Speak the truth in love

1. Search our hearts, O Lord, and if there is any unforgiveness, bring it to our minds and help us to release it now, we pray.
2. Rather than harbour resentment against anyone who has wronged us, O Lord, give us the grace to speak to them the truth in love.
3. Holy Spirit, develop more and more within us, the *agapé* love of God, we pray.

4. Give us the wisdom, O Lord, as to when to simply overlook an offence and forget about it, and when we need to speak to that person to bring it to their attention, so it will not fester within us.
5. Give us the love of God that enables us to "cover a multitude of sins" and so for us not to take offence needlessly.

 Leviticus 19:18
Love your neighbour

1. Open our eyes daily, Holy Spirit, to those people who you want us to see as our 'neighbour', and therefore ones you want us to be a blessing to at this time.
2. Since this is a command and not a suggestion, help us, Holy Spirit, to become so like Christ, that this becomes our lifestyle.
3. Lord, help us to show a love that is patient and kind; that does not envy, and is not proud, boastful or rude.
4. Lord, help us to show a love that is not self-seeking; is not easily angered, and keeps no record of wrongs.
5. Lord, help us to show a love that does not delight in evil, but rejoices with the truth, that always protects, always trusts, always hopes and always perseveres.

 Leviticus 19:19
Keeping God's decrees

1. Give us obedient hearts, O Lord, that delight to do your will.
2. Help us to keep our old fallen nature firmly put to death, and to allow it no opportunity to rise up again.
3. Deal with any areas of rebellion in our hearts against the ways or the will of God, Holy Spirit, and give us the determination to root them out permanently.
4. May our will be in line with your will, O Lord, and where it is not, help us today to bring it into line with what you desire.

5. As we read your Word, O Lord, may the Holy Spirit show us any way we are not adhering to a life of holiness, so we may change anything that needs to change.

16th Leviticus 19:20-22
Sexual integrity

1. Lord, we pray for your Church, that no matter what the pressures from the world may be, we would always act with total integrity in all matters to do with sex and sexuality.
2. Help us not to conform to the standards of the world in these matters, but rather to conform to the standards of holiness you require from us, we pray.
3. We pray for all the young people of our nation, O Lord, that there would be a growing realisation that sexual permissiveness leads only to unhappiness in the long run.
4. We pray for those in Government and places of leadership in our nation, that you would help them realise the great harm that sexual permissiveness is doing to our society, and cause them to change their policies.
5. We take authority over the unclean spirits that are operating freely over our nation, and bind them in Jesus' Name.

17th Leviticus 19:23-25
Fruitfulness (1)

1. Lord, as we seek first the Kingdom of God and your righteousness, add to us all that we need in our lives, we pray.
2. We pray that you would make our employment fruitful, O Lord.
3. We pray that you would make all our businesses fruitful, O God.
4. We pray you would make our family and social lives emotionally and spiritually fruitful, O Lord.
5. We pray that you would make our ministries fruitful, O Lord.

Leviticus 19:23-25
Fruitfulness (2)

1. Give us the desire to so seek after our God, that we overflow with every aspect of the fruit of the Spirit, we pray.
2. Make us fruitful by leading others to Christ, we pray.
3. Lord, grow us as your church both spiritually and numerically, we pray.
4. Make us fruitful with every gift of the Holy Spirit operating in our midst, we pray.
5. Lord, may we your people carry such an anointing of your Spirit, that in all we do we become the head and not the tail.

Leviticus 19:26
No occult activities

1. Forgive any of us who have had dealings with occult activities in the past, O God, and we renounce, right now, any such ties from the past.
2. We pray for those who follow Christ, but who still read their horoscopes; open their eyes and set them free, we pray.
3. We pray for all those who have had dealings with tarot cards; deliver them from any bondage, O God.
4. For all those in our midst still suffering as a result of involvement in the past with witchcraft or related activities, help, deliver and set them free, we pray.
5. For all those suffering as a consequence of being the subject of curses or generational curses, help, deliver and set them free, we pray.

20th Leviticus 19:27-28
Good stewards of our physical bodies

1. Cause us to remember that our bodies are the temple of the Holy Spirit, and may we be good stewards of them.
2. Lord, may we not abuse our bodies through gluttony.
3. Lord, may we not misuse our bodies through drink, drugs or cigarettes, and set free all those in your church who are in bondage to any of these things.
4. Lord, may we not misuse our bodies through an immoral lifestyle, and convict all who are doing so, we pray.
5. Help us to carry ourselves in such a way that is fitting for sons and daughters of the living God.

 21st Leviticus 19:29
Living in purity (1)

1. Keep us from fornication, O Lord.
2. Keep us from adultery, O Lord.
3. Keep us from all forms of unnatural sexual activity, we pray.
4. Thank you, Lord Jesus, for the robes of righteousness you clothe us with when we give our lives to you; teach us to seek after practical holiness, and so honour your Name.
5. Give us clean hands and pure hearts, O Lord, that enable us to approach you with confidence.

 22nd Leviticus 19:29
Living in purity (2)

1. Lord, the unsaved around us, who do not know you, cannot live according to the principles of your Kingdom; use us to save and change them, so that they can know the joy of pursuing a life of holiness with Christ.

2. For any believer we know, who struggles with temptation regarding any kind of immorality in their life, help and deliver them, that they may be at peace, Lord, we pray.
3. We pray for any individuals we know, who are in bondage to pornography; deliver them, and help them find the true love that comes from knowing Christ.
4. Lord, give us discernment as to what is right and what is wrong to watch on TV, films and the Internet.
5. Give us the power and determination to take captive every impure thought and make them obedient to Christ, we pray.

 Leviticus 19:30
Revere the Lord

1. Cause us to always to give you honour, O Lord, through our words, our thoughts and our actions.
2. Teach us the fear of the Lord, which is the beginning of wisdom, and cause it to change us profoundly.
3. May our very lives be lived out in reverence to you, O Lord, knowing that our bodies are your dwelling place.
4. Lord, you have said that if we love you, we will keep your commandments; may our actions match our words, we pray.
5. May we honour your Word, O God, and demonstrate it by not only reading it, but also by always putting it into action.

 Leviticus 19:31
Shun mediums

1. We pray for all in our midst who have been left troubled by visiting a medium; set them free from every bondage, we pray.
2. For those we know, who are addicted to psychic telephone lines; deliver them, we pray.
3. For those we know, who still have their palms read or fortunes told; open their eyes to the truth and set them free, we pray.

4. We pray for all the young people we know, who are tempted to use ouija boards; keep them from such folly, O Lord.

5. We pray for all the mediums that live in our area, O Lord; save them, and cause them to turn to the true Source of spiritual power.

 **25th** Leviticus 19:32
Respect the elderly

1. May we be a people who always show respect for the elderly, O Lord.

2. Let us be a people who have respect for those placed in authority over us, we pray, knowing that this is your will.

3. We pray for all the grandparents in the church and outside the church, that you would bless and help them, and cause their wisdom to be passed on to the next generation.

4. Lord, we pray for all the pastors and elders of our church, that you would help and bless them in the work they do in leading the church.

5. We pray for all those in the House of Commons and in the House of Lords; guide and lead them in godly and wise decisions, we pray.

 26th Leviticus 19:33
Treat all with the same kindness

1. We pray for all Muslims we know; save them, and let them know the joy of salvation through Christ.

2. We pray for all the Hindus we know; save them, and let them know the joy of eternal life in Jesus.

3. We pray for all the Sikhs we know; save them, and help them know the joy of finding Christ as Saviour.

4. We pray for all the Buddhists we know; save them, and help them find the true and living God.

5. We pray for those from other religions that do not know Christ; save them, and reveal yourself to them as Saviour, Lord Jesus.

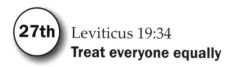

27th Leviticus 19:34
Treat everyone equally

1. We pray for all the unsaved people we know from the continent of Asia; save them, O Lord.
2. We pray for all the unsaved people we know from the continent of Africa; save them, O Lord.
3. We pray for all the unsaved people we know from the continents of Europe and Antarctica; save them, O Lord.
4. We pray for all the unsaved people we know from the continent of the Americas; save them, O Lord.
5. We pray for all the unsaved people we know from Australasia and all the island countries; save them, O Lord.

28th Leviticus 19:35-36
No cheating (1)

1. May we be honest in all our dealings, we pray.
2. May we be honest in all our dealings with the Government - national or local, O Lord.
3. May we always be faithful to adhere to all the promises and agreements we make, O God.
4. May we always be honest in regard to all our academic work or other tests we need to pass.
5. Let honesty be so much part of our nature that we would not even have to pause to think which is the right path to take.

29th Leviticus 19:35-36
No cheating (2)

1. Convict us when we sin, Holy Spirit, and give us the courage and grace to confess whenever we fall.
2. Whenever we are handling money, O Lord, may we be scrupulously honest.
3. In our places of work, O God, may we never take anything without permission, nor take advantage of our employers.
4. Help us to be honest with our time in our places of work, and to give our full effort in accordance with the contracts of work we have agreed to.
5. Help us not to rob you, O God, but to give of our finances in accordance with your will.

30th Leviticus 19:37
Keeping God's decrees

1. Teach us not merely to be converts, but to be true disciples of Jesus, following you in all your ways, O Lord.
2. Holy Spirit, continue to operate upon our hearts and our consciences, guiding us in every area of our lives to follow all your ways carefully.
3. Let us be good students of your Word, O God, so that we know what you would have us do in any situation, because we know the Bible's teaching.
4. Write your laws upon our hearts, O Lord, that we would know the right decision to make in any and every situation.
5. May we always live as ambassadors for the King of kings, such that we can say: "Follow my example, as I follow the example of Christ."

December

God's Gift of Jesus

Luke Chapters 1 & 2
Matthew Chapters 1 & 2

The Bible shows us that the birth of Jesus occurred at the exact point in human history that God had planned, to be able to accomplish his pre-ordained plan of salvation for the world.

He had prepared the world for the rapid spread of the Gospel:

> **The birth of Jesus occurred at the exact point in human history that God had planned**

1. The Jews had been scattered throughout the world in the centuries before, and, as a consequence, there was a synagogue in every major town and city in different countries. This made it easy for the apostles, such as Paul, to go straight to the synagogue, where the Jews would be familiar with the Old Testament and the prophecies of the coming Messiah. Paul preached the Gospel 'first for the Jew and then for the Gentile' (Romans 1:16). His strategy, wherever possible, was to win Jews

for Christ, who had an understanding of the Lord; establish a church, and then move on, leaving the elders behind to shepherd the flock in the new church.

> **At just the right moment, the Christ ... was born into the world he came to save**

2. The Empire, established briefly by Alexander the Great some 300 years before Christ, left its legacy of an international language, namely Greek, which was spoken throughout the known world. This made it easy for the apostles to travel from country to country preaching the Good News in Greek, without having to learn every local language. The New Testament was also written in Greek, and widely read and understood.

3. The Roman Empire, in existence before and during the life of Christ, had been instrumental in laying roads of excellent quality, connecting all its major cities, and making travel from city to city very easy. The presence of its soldiers on every street corner ensured the world at that time was at peace, thereby also allowing easy movement around the countries of the Empire, where the churches could be established in every area.

So, at just the right moment, the Christ, promised by the prophets of old, was born into the world he came to save. His miraculous birth, as the Holy Spirit overshadowed the young virgin Mary, ensured this 'last Adam' would be born without any of the taint of sin inherited by the human race through the first Adam. Jesus the Christ could therefore, as a perfect human being (as well as being fully divine), be able to offer himself as the perfect Sacrifice. Or, in the words of John the Baptist: "Behold the Lamb of God, who takes away the sins of the world." This Christmas, the greatest gift you could receive, or give by telling someone else, is the eternal life that comes through faith in Jesus Christ.

• • • • • • • • • • • • • • • • • • •

Luke 1:1-4
Being certain of what we have been taught

1. Lord, help us to study your Word with diligence, and give us daily a sincere desire to learn more of your ways.
2. Holy Spirit, teach us as we read the Bible to correctly discern and understand the truth, and then to put it into practice in our daily lives.
3. Guard our hearts and minds against every subtle attack of the enemy on our faith, that would seek to cause doubts and uncertainties to trouble our minds.
4. May your Word, O Lord, be the solid foundation upon which we build our lives, and from which we may minister effectively and helpfully into the lives of others.
5. We pray for all those individuals we know, who teach your Word, whether to children, youth or adults; may they produce lasting fruit in those who hear them.

 Luke 1:5-7
Upright in the sight of God

1. Search our hearts, O Lord, and reveal to us any areas of our lives that are not helping us to be upright in your sight, so we can change in those areas.
2. Give us a heart to be obedient at all times and in all ways to your commands, so that we may grow in the process of becoming more like Jesus.
3. Help me today, Heavenly Father, to become a little more like your Son, Jesus.
4. Help us today to be able to make a difference in the lives of others, to encourage and to help them on the pathway of becoming more like Jesus.
5. May the way we go about our daily tasks at home, outside and at work cause non-believers to ask: Why are you the way you are? Enable us to point them to Jesus.

3rd Luke 1:8-10
Worship and prayer

1. Help us always to realise and remember, O Lord, that we are created to worship you and bring you glory, and when we do so, we can rise above our circumstances.
2. May the busyness of our daily routine never crowd out the times we need to spend in your presence, where we can minister to you in worship and prayer, and where you can minister to us.
3. Since we no longer need to bring animal sacrifices to you, may we be generous in those spiritual sacrifices we bring to you of prayer, worship, thanksgiving and praise.
4. May we not neglect joining with the assembly of your people in our collective acts of worship, but rather come to be a blessing to you and to others.
5. As we worship you right now in spirit and in truth, and lift our voices in praise, O Lord, fill us with your joy and your peace.

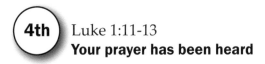

4th Luke 1:11-13
Your prayer has been heard

1. Help us to believe and never to doubt that you are a God for whom nothing is impossible.
2. We bring before you now the prayers concerning our deepest needs, believing that you can do all things.
3. Thank you, Lord, that we can enter boldly into your very presence at all times. May we not neglect that great and wonderful privilege.
4. We thank you for every prayer we have brought to you and have seen you answer. May we never be shy of sharing testimonies of answers to prayer, that you may be glorified and others may be built up.
5. Speak to us, Lord, as we wait upon you in prayer, that we may know and walk in your perfect will for our lives.

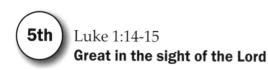

5th Luke 1:14-15
Great in the sight of the Lord

1. Like John the Baptist, may we be the kind of people who, because of our Christlike nature, bring joy and delight to others in the things we do and say.
2. Lord, just as you had a perfect plan prepared for John's life, so you have a perfect plan for ours. In our free will, help us to make the right choices, so that your plan for our individual lives may be fulfilled.
3. Holy Spirit, help us to dream big dreams of what we can do through Christ, and give us the courage to seek to see them fulfilled.
4. Fill us afresh today with your Holy Spirit, O God, and enable us to constantly move in the anointing and power of your Spirit within us.
5. Help us not to be content with the mediocre, but rather help us rise to our full potential in Christ, making a difference in the world around us.

6th Luke 1:16-17
In the spirit and power of Elijah

1. May we, like John, be people who can turn people's hearts to the Lord, and right now we pray for the backsliders and non-Christians that we know; turn their hearts back to you, O Lord.
2. Cause us to walk closely with you, O Lord, so that you may be able to work through us in the power of your Holy Spirit.
3. Cause us, as a church, to walk so closely to you, O God, that you are able to manifest the power of your Holy Spirit in our midst continually.
4. We pray for a greater manifestation of your power in our midst, O Lord. May we continually be stepping out with the faith that can move mountains.

5. We pray for all the churches up and down the land to experience a fresh visitation of the Holy Spirit, and with a release of signs and wonders that draw people to Christ.

7th Luke 1:18-20
Unbelief

1. Guard our hearts against unbelief, O Lord, so that we do not sin against you in that way.
2. Where our faith is weak, make it strong; where there is discouragement, gives us encouragement; when we have doubts, help us to dispel them.
3. We pray for those we know, who are going through a time of doubting; help them, and help us to give them strength to stop doubting and believe.
4. O God, who created and who sustains the vast universe; who raised the dead and who can do all things, help us to grasp your limitless power and never disbelieve your Word.
5. Water the seeds of our faith and belief, so that they can become strong and mighty in God.

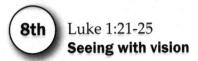

8th Luke 1:21-25
Seeing with vision

1. Since those without a vision can perish, give each of us your vision for our individual lives, and a heart of courage to see the vision fulfilled.
2. We pray for all the church leaders in our locality, that each would hear clearly from God, and would know and pursue the vision that God desires them to outwork.
3. We pray for the vision of our own church; let each member get hold of it, understand it, and be part of its fulfilment to the glory of God.

4. We pray for revival in the church, for each member to be disciples, and for us as individuals and as a church to bring godly change to our communities.
5. Keep before our eyes, O Lord, a vision of the cross of Jesus, and may it be our motivation in all that we think and do.

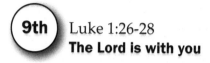

9th Luke 1:26-28
The Lord is with you

1. Thank you, our Father, that we are each highly favoured by you, and are the object of your intense love, as demonstrated by the cross of Jesus.
2. When the circumstances of life seem to be close to overwhelming us, help us never to forget your promise that you will never leave us nor forsake us.
3. When we are tempted to say or do the wrong thing, even when no one is watching, help us at that time to remember that the Lord is with us.
4. We pray for those we know, who are feeling alone for whatever reason; help us today to show them something of the love of Jesus by something we can do or say.
5. Thank you, Heavenly Father, that you are with us and not against us; help us to remember that those who are for us are greater than those against us, and that greater is he who is within us, than he that is in the world.

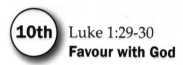

10th Luke 1:29-30
Favour with God

1. Lord, receiving your divine favour is worth more than the riches of the whole world. Grant us your favour in our individual lives.
2. We pray for your divine favour in the life of our church; graciously lead, guide, rebuke and correct us, so that we may follow your perfect ways for us.

3. We pray for your divine favour in our prayer lives, as individuals and as a church, that you would show us how to pray with insight, power and effectiveness in all areas of our lives, work, families and ministries.
4. Show your favour on your churches up and down this land, O Lord. Turn the hearts of your people back to you wholeheartedly, and cause your Church to be a powerful agent for change for the good.
5. Show your divine favour on our nation once again, O God. Turn the hearts of those in positions of power and government away from ungodliness and back to your ways.

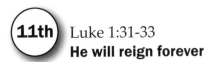 Luke 1:31-33
He will reign forever

1. Lord, let your Kingdom have full reign in our individual lives, as we humble ourselves in acknowledgement of your lordship over our lives.
2. Reign over your church, rise up in our midst and move in mighty power amongst us in salvation, deliverance, healings, signs and wonders.
3. Rise up in our Discipleship Cell meetings, moving in power to save people and multiply in numbers.
4. Let your Kingdom come and your will be done in our church, in our families, and in the communities we live and work amongst.
5. Rise up, O Lord, and let all your enemies be scattered, pulling down every spiritual stronghold that seeks to oppose the building of your Kingdom in the hearts and lives of men and women.

 Luke 1:34-36
The Holy Spirit will come upon you

1. Holy Spirit, come and fill me right now, and enable me to speak in a new divinely-inspired language that will revolutionise my prayer life.

2. We pray for all in the church who are not yet baptised in the Holy Spirit; may they continue to ask, seek and knock until they have received this good gift from the Father.
3. Give us the desire, O Lord, to stir up the flames within each of us, so that we may burn with the passion and fire of the Holy Spirit.
4. Heavenly Father, cause there to be such an outpouring of your Holy Spirit up and down this land, that the churches will be turned upside down, and that our cities, towns and villages will turn to Jesus Christ as Saviour.
5. Holy Spirit, just as you birthed something supernatural in the body of Mary, birth something new in our lives today, as we hunger and thirst after the things of God.

 Luke 1:37
Nothing is impossible for God

1. Lord, we are often so slow to believe; forgive our doubts and strengthen our faith.
2. Help us to use the faith we already have in such a way as to be able to move any form of 'mountain' that stands before us this day.
3. As a church, give us a collective spiritual strength, as we stand together and believe for the impossible in all situations that you are leading us to pray about.
4. Just as, in God, one can chase a thousand and two can chase ten thousand, as we grow in faith, may we see the power of prayer multiply in the same way.
5. We pray for those we know today, who are on the verge of giving up because their faith has evaporated; we uphold them before you now, and ask that you would help them to understand that nothing is impossible for God.

14th Luke 1:38
The Lord's servant

1. We have accepted you as our Saviour; help us conquer our rebellious natures, so that we truly make you Lord of every part of our lives.
2. Give each of us a humble heart that is the sign of a true servant of the Lord.
3. When you speak to us by your Spirit within us about any situation in our lives, may we not close our ears in rebellion, but be open to be obedient.
4. Lord, right now we surrender every area of our lives to you. If there is anything we are holding back from you, show us, so we may surrender it to you now.
5. Teach us to learn the secret of greatness in God, which is not to trust in our own strength, talents or abilities, but to allow you to raise us up as we bow before you.

15th Luke 1:39-45
Blessed of God

1. Lord, we give you thanks for all your goodness towards us, shown in so many ways, and want to tell you that we are grateful for your many blessings.
2. Teach us to be grateful people, and not ones who are always quick to grumble and complain.
3. We pray for those Christians we know, who are struggling for one reason or another, and are not conscious of your blessing, Lord. Help them to overcome, we pray.
4. We pray for all your people who struggle in countries where the economy is poor. Meet their every need - physically, socially, emotionally and spiritually - and may their faith be a powerful witness to the non-believers in their countries.

5. We pray for all those Christians who are living in countries where they are persecuted; bless them in the midst of their fiery trials, we pray, O Lord.

Luke 1:46-56
Glorifying God

1. May our individual lives bring glory to you, O Lord.
2. May the way we conduct ourselves in our places of work bring glory to you, O Lord.
3. May the way we live in our family homes - as sons, daughters, fathers, mothers, brothers and sisters, husbands and wives - bring glory to you, O Lord.
4. May the way we conduct ourselves in church and amongst the household of fellow believers bring glory to you, O Lord.
5. If there are any parts of our lives that are not bringing you glory, because we are not truly keeping to your ways, convict us and help us to change, O Lord.

Luke 1:57-66
An unusual child

1. Lord, we pray for our children; help us to be such good examples of how to live for Jesus, that they will grow to want to have the same experience themselves of knowing and living for you.
2. We pray for all the children in our church, that those who do not yet know you will come to do so, and that those who do, will continue to grow in you.
3. Cause our children not only to come to know you at a young age, O Lord, but also to receive the baptism in the Holy Spirit.
4. Raise up our children to become ones who know their destiny in Christ, and who are able to move powerfully in the knowledge of God and in the gifts of the Holy Spirit.

5. We pray for all parents, and all those who teach the children in the Children's Ministries; may they wisely impart a knowledge and a thirst for God, that will be a solid foundation for the children to build their spiritual lives upon.

 18th Luke 1:67-79
Giving people the knowledge of salvation

1. Lord, help us to understand - and put in the right order - our priorities in life, and to understand that we are all here on earth to be ministers for Christ.
2. Give us a heart for the lost: to pray for them, to love them, to speak to them about salvation, and to lead them to the Lord.
3. We bring before you now, Jesus, those three people closest to us (our 'Prayer of Three'), who as yet do not know you as Saviour and Lord. Save them, we pray.
4. Mobilise all the people in our church, O God, to witness boldly, effectively, and in the power and strength of the Holy Spirit, seeing people saved, healed and transformed.
5. Let your Church rise up in the United Kingdom in the power and spirit of John the Baptist and of Elijah, as a voice crying in the wilderness, "Prepare the way of the Lord," and cause this nation to repent and turn to God.

 19th Luke 1:80
Becoming strong in spirit

1. Help us daily to grow a little more in the Lord, so that we become ever stronger in spirit.
2. Lord, our spirits may be willing, but often our flesh seems weak; help us to overcome the weakness of our human nature.
3. Give us the wisdom to spend our time on things that edify and build up our spiritual lives, and not on things that will pull them down.

4. Give us the desire and motivation to ensure we always spend time with you each day in prayer, O Heavenly Father.
5. May we not neglect the daily reading of your Word, without which we cannot grow strong in spirit.

20th Luke 2:1-7
No room for Jesus

1. Lord, if there are any areas of our lives where we are shutting you out, and saying there is no room for you there, forgive us and cause us to change, we pray.
2. We pray for our schools up and down the land, which seek to shut you out, Lord Jesus, or replace you with the wisdom of men; forgive and bring the changes necessary to give you the place you deserve.
3. We pray for all our universities that oppose or make life difficult for the spreading of the Gospel; bring the changes necessary to those in positions of authority, that you may have the prominence you deserve, Lord Jesus.
4. In all institutions in our nation and national life, where godless men seek to squeeze you out, O Lord, rise up in power, and bring the change that is needed.
5. We pray for our Parliament, and for all the legislation that it has passed and seeks to pass that has the effect of pushing out biblical values and principles; raise up godly men and women, who will be led by your Spirit to pass righteous laws.

21st Luke 2:8-10
Bringing Good News

1. Lord, give us words and attitudes so that we are people who always speak graciously, and can edify those we speak to.
2. May the way we live out our lives be such that others can see we have been changed by the Good News of Jesus Christ.

3. Lead us today, O Lord, to somebody who you want to hear the Good News of Jesus from our lips.
4. Enable us to be the peacemakers you want us to be, and not troublemakers, so that we are always 'good news' to others.
5. Thank you, Lord Jesus, for the day when we heard the Good News that you could save us from our sins; and thank you for doing so.

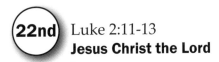

22nd Luke 2:11-13
Jesus Christ the Lord

1. Thank you, O God, that the Name 'Jesus' shows us the humanity of our Saviour, who understands our every situation because he has lived as we live. Give us your peace, we pray.
2. We thank you, O God, that the Name 'Christ' shows us that Jesus is the Messiah, the Anointed One, who is able to do all things; help us not to worry or be anxious, we pray.
3. Thank you, O Lord, that the Name 'Lord' shows us that you rule over all powers and dominions, whether visible or invisible, and we are therefore totally safe in your hands.
4. Thank you, Lord Jesus, that your birth showed the beginning of the end for the 'prince of this world,' whom you defeated on our behalf through the cross. We worship you.
5. We give you glory this day, O Lord, for who you are; what you have done; what you are doing now, and all that you are going to do.

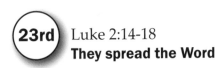

23rd Luke 2:14-18
They spread the Word

1. Lord, we pray for all ministers in churches up and down our land; give them the grace and courage to boldly preach the uncompromising Word of God at all times.

2. We pray for all ministers in countries, whose governments are hostile to the preaching of the Gospel; give them courage, grace and boldness to preach your Word with the wisdom that comes from the Holy Spirit.
3. We pray for all missionaries throughout the world, who are seeking to spread the Good News of Jesus Christ; give them grace, and make them effective witnesses for Jesus Christ.
4. We pray for all the tracts that are distributed on our streets; by your Spirit, O Lord, cause people to be arrested by their message; be convicted of sin, and turn to Christ.
5. We pray for all believers that are broadcasting the Gospel to non-Christian lands via radio and television; may they be able to reach those for Christ who would otherwise remain unreached.

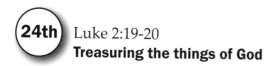 **24th** Luke 2:19-20
Treasuring the things of God

1. When we read your Word, O Lord, let your truths be deposited in our hearts and remain there, seasoning every part of our lives.
2. Those occasions when you have spoken to us in different ways, O Lord, may we not forget what you have said, but treasure your words in our hearts.
3. Lord, remember the things you have promised us as individuals, and watch over your Word to perform it at the right time.
4. Since the words that come from our mouths reflect the contents of our hearts, enable us to deposit nothing but the goodness of your Word in our hearts, O Lord.
5. Teach us to value and to know the difference between true, spiritual treasure, and that which has no eternal value.

25th Matthew 1:18-25
Joseph did what the Lord commanded

1. Thank you, Heavenly Father, for the priceless gift of your Son, Jesus.
2. Thank you, Lord Jesus, for choosing to leave Heaven's glory, to join your divine nature with our human nature, and to be obedient, even to death on the cross, so that we might know the salvation of God.
3. Thank you, Lord, for the obedience of the earthly parents you found in Joseph and Mary; may we be equally quick to obey your commands.
4. Since you have said that "obedience is better than sacrifice," teach us, Heavenly Father, to understand the critical importance of being obedient to you.
5. Come and reign in our hearts in full measure this day and every day, Lord Jesus.

26th Matthew 2:1-12
Gifts for Jesus

1. As the Magi brought you a gift of gold, Lord, may we be equally generous with our giving to you and to your work.
2. As the Magi brought you a gift of frankincense, to be used in worship, may we freely bring you our sacrifices of worship in spirit and in truth.
3. As the Magi brought you a gift of myrrh, an ointment used in burials, may we continually remember that the cost of your coming into this world was the suffering of the cross on our behalf.
4. May we be people, O Lord, who delight in our giving, and not ones who selfishly hold back.
5. Give us generous hearts to those in need who are less fortunate than ourselves, and the wisdom when and how to help them.

27th Matthew 2:13-18
Opposing God

1. Have mercy, O Lord, on all those in positions of political authority, who use their powers to oppose you and your ways.
2. We pray for all those governments in Asian countries, that oppose the preaching of the Gospel and conversions to Christ; frustrate their opposition, O Lord.
3. We pray for those governments in Middle Eastern countries, that oppose the preaching of the Gospel and conversions to Christ; frustrate their opposition, O God.
4. We pray for those governments in African countries and European countries, that oppose the preaching of the Gospel and conversions to Christ; frustrate their actions, O Lord.
5. We pray for all governments in the Americas and island nations, that seek to oppose the preaching of the Gospel and conversions to Christ; frustrate their opposition, O Lord.

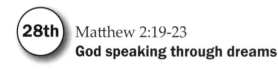

28th Matthew 2:19-23
God speaking through dreams

1. Lord, we pray that you would speak to us in dreams and visions, and also give us the understanding of what you are saying to us through them.
2. We thank you for the way you often appear to Muslims and others in dreams and visions, revealing that Jesus is Lord and Saviour, and causing them to give their lives to you; do it more and more, O God.
3. Give us dreams of the future that are inspired by the Holy Spirit, and the wisdom, patience and perseverance to walk closely to you until we see them fulfilled.
4. Lord, you promised in your Word that "your sons and your daughters will prophesy; your old men will dream dreams; your young men will see visions." Pour out your Spirit on us afresh in our day, O Lord.

5. Reveal to us more and more of yourself, O God, and give us the wisdom to understand and respond to your revelation.

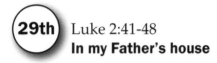

29th Luke 2:41-48
In my Father's house

1. May we love to be in your presence, in the company of your people, and in your house seeking you, O Father.
2. May we not be negligent to meet together in your house, O Lord, and not to let any small excuse cause us to miss or forsake our times of corporate worship in church.
3. Thank you, O Lord, for the freedom we currently enjoy to be able to meet together to worship you; may we not abuse our freedom.
4. We pray for your presence to so fill your house on Sundays and at other times we meet together, that everyone present will be conscious of the life-changing presence and power of a living God.
5. Give us listening ears and a heart that provides good soil for the seed of your Word to take root and produce fruit in our lives.

30th Luke 2:50
Obedient to his parents

1. Give the parents in our church divine wisdom in the bringing up of their children in our modern society, where godlessness is so prevalent, we pray.
2. Keep our children from the spirit of disobedience, that is at work so blatantly in this world.
3. May our parents not exasperate their children, but instead bring them up in the training and instruction of the Lord.
4. Help the parents in the church to bring their children up, such that each child honours their father and mother.

5. We pray for all the children of non-Christian parents; help them to raise their children, so that they have respect for all forms of godly authority.

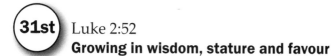

31st Luke 2:52
Growing in wisdom, stature and favour

1. Lord, you have told us that the fear of the Lord is the beginning of wisdom; cause us to have a godly fear that will provide us with divine wisdom.
2. Give us wisdom in all the affairs of our daily lives, so that we always make the right choices.
3. As we grow spiritually, enable us to be people who can minister wisely into the lives of others, as we grow in spiritual stature.
4. We pray for all those who hold positions of leadership in our church at whatever level, that you would cause them to grow in wisdom, stature and favour, O Lord.
5. We pray for all those in our church, who are engaged in ministries of every nature; cause them to grow in wisdom, stature and divine favour, as they seek to serve you, O God.

If you have read this book and you do not have a personal relationship with God through trusting in Jesus, or you are not sure if you have, and so you do not have an assurance of your sins being forgiven, then here (opposite) is a prayer you can pray.

If you mean it from your heart, God will hear and enable you to be born-again and become a child of his, enabling you to have a personal and intimate relationship with him, both now and forever.

. . . .

If you have prayed this prayer for the first time, we would encourage you to seek a Bible-believing church near you.

For help, you can telephone our 24/7 Prayer Centre on 020 8799 2199 (or from abroad: 44 20 8799 2199).

" Heavenly Father,
I thank you that you love me.
I realise that I have fallen short
of your perfect standards
and that this has separated me from you
and kept me from knowing you personally.
I thank you that, in Jesus,
all my sins can be forgiven.
I acknowledge all the things
I have done wrong
and now desire to turn away from them.
I believe that Jesus Christ is the Son of God
who came from heaven to this earth
to die for my sins
and rise again from the dead,
demonstrating that he really is God.
I now ask you, Jesus,
to be my Saviour and my Lord.
Please come into my life
and change me from the inside out
and enable me to have
a personal relationship with you
from this moment and forever. **"**
Amen.

REVIVAL PRAYERS - Volume 1

About the Author

Richard and Rajinder Buxton have been working together in ministry for over 30 years, having given up their former professions as a solicitor and a nurse, respectively, to enter Bible College. After a few years in pastoral ministry, they served for many years overseas as missionaries with the Elim International Missions Department.

Working first in Tanzania in East Africa, Richard's brief was to set up and run a full-time Bible College for the training of pastors and church workers. After handing the work over to trained local ministers, they left Tanzania, and moved to Malaysia in South East Asia, where they worked with Sikh, Hindu and Chinese communities. It was from here, in 1997, that they heeded God's call to come to the UK as pastors in Ealing Christian Centre.

With ECC's congregation of around 100 different nationalities, Richard and Rajinder believe God has carefully planned their ministry from the beginning. He allowed them to acquire valuable experience in Europe, Africa and Asia in order to equip them for leadership in ECC, with people from diverse ethnic backgrounds as "One family of many nations, proclaiming one Gospel through many disciples."

Richard and Rajinder have a passion to see revival in the church, in our communities and in our nation. Their desire is to see all members of the church discipled, equipped, released for service, and active in ministry as ministers of Christ, both in the UK and indeed to different nations of the world, carrying the message of the Gospel in the power of the Holy Spirit.

Rajinder is originally from Malaysia, and was born into a staunch Sikh family, the daughter of a Sikh priest. She came to know Christ at the age of 15, and moved to England a few years after this. A passionate evangelist, Rajinder's background plays an important role in her desire to see many people of all nations saved through the power of the Gospel, and to witness signs and wonders and the power of God.

As a means of accomplishing the vision for revival, a 24-hour ECC Prayer Centre was set up in June 2002, where intercessors continuously pray for revival in the church and in our community, whilst also interceding for people's needs. The Centre has been running 24 hours a day ever since.

•••••••••••••••••••

IN NEED OF PRAYER?

Call our confidential prayer line for **any** need:

Bereavement • Loneliness
Sickness • Health issues
Job pressures • Crisis
Addiction • Family worries
Salvation • Re-commitment

24/7 PRAYER CENTRE
(Established June 2002)

Open 24 hours a day
7 days a week

020 8799 2199
(From abroad: 44 20 8799 2199)